THE SILVER STATE BUCKET LIST
100 DESTINATIONS YOU MUST VISIT

NEVADA

TRAVEL GUIDE

DIANA L.
MITCHELL

Table of Contents

II

III

Dear reader, thanks a lot for purchasing my book.

To help you plan your trip even more efficiently, I have included an interactive map powered by Google My Maps.

To access it, scan the QR code below.

Happy travelling!

A Note to Our Valued Readers

Thank you for choosing this travel guide as your companion for exploring the world.

I want to take a moment to address a concern you might have regarding the absence of photographs in this book.

As an independent author and publisher, I strive to deliver high-quality, informative content at an affordable price.

Including photographs in a printed book, however, presents significant challenges. Licensing high-quality images can be extremely costly, and unfortunately, I have no control over the print quality of images within the book.

Because these guides are printed and shipped by Amazon, I am unable to review the final print quality before they reach your hands.

So, rather than risk compromising your reading experience with subpar visuals, I've chosen to focus on providing detailed, insightful content that will help you make the most of your travels.

While this guide may not contain photos, it's packed with valuable information, insider tips, and recommendations to ensure you have an enriching and memorable journey.

Additionally, there's an interactive map powered by Google My Maps—an essential tool to help you plan your trip.

I encourage you to supplement your reading with online resources where you can find up-to-date images and visuals of the destinations covered in this guide.

I hope you find this book a helpful and inspiring resource as you embark on your next adventure.

Thank you for your understanding and support.

Safe travels,

Diana

Introduction

Welcome to *Nevada Travel Guide*, your comprehensive guide to exploring the diverse and vibrant tapestry of destinations across the Silver State. From the electrifying streets of Las Vegas, where entertainment reigns supreme, to the tranquil beauty of the Great Basin National Park, this guide is a treasure trove for travelers seeking both iconic and hidden gems of Nevada.

Our adventure begins in Reno and Western Nevada, a region steeped in rich history and natural allure. Stroll the picturesque Lake Tahoe shoreline, uncover the past at the Historic Fourth Ward School Museum in Virginia City, or hike the serene trails of Galena Creek Park. Each destination, from the iconic Reno Arch to the lush Washoe Lake State Park, offers a unique slice of the West's charm and heritage.

Venturing north, we discover Northern Nevada, a landscape teeming with rugged beauty and boundless outdoor adventure. Marvel at the expansive views from the Ruby Mountains, indulge in the natural hot springs of Elko, or explore the historic pathways of the California Trail. Northern Nevada is a sanctuary for nature enthusiasts and history aficionados alike, boasting destinations like the Cowboy Arts & Gear Museum and the remote wilderness of Jarbidge.

Central Nevada calls with its intriguing mix of historical intrigue and mystical landscapes. Explore the quirky International Car Forest of The Last Church, step back in time at the historic Eureka Opera House, or witness the ancient Toquima Cave Art. The region offers a blend of cultural and natural wonders, from the ghostly ruins of Stokes Castle to the serene expanses of Great Basin National Park.

Our journey culminates in Las Vegas and Southern Nevada, where the vibrant energy of modern entertainment intersects with the tranquility of natural landscapes. Wander through the historic Boulder City District, revel in the excitement of high-stakes games at the Bellagio, or find peace among the dramatic red rock formations of the Valley of Fire State Park. This region is a dynamic hub of excitement and beauty, from the bustling Las Vegas Strip to the tranquil waters of Lake Mead.

Nevada Travel Guide is more than a mere travel guide; it's an invitation to immerse yourself in the rich tapestry of Nevada's beauty, history, and entertainment. Each of these meticulously selected 100 destinations promises an authentic and memorable exploration of the Silver State. So pack your bags, ignite your curiosity, and prepare to delve into Nevada like never before!

About Nevada

Landscape of Nevada

In *Nevada Travel Guide*, we delve deep not only into the myriad attractions but also into the state's diverse and captivating landscapes that embody the varied natural beauty of the American West. Each chapter of this guide is a journey through the distinct terrains and natural wonders that make Nevada a unique gem in the rugged landscape of the United States.

High Desert Vistas: Northern Nevada's Expansive Beauty

Northern Nevada is defined by its vast high desert landscapes. From the arid, sagebrush-dotted expanses around Reno to the striking geological formations of Pyramid Lake, this region offers a striking meeting of earth and sky. Historic landmarks such as the Virginia City Historic District stand as echoes of the mining boom, and the culture in these parts is deeply influenced by both indigenous heritage and the Old West pioneering spirit.

Urban Oasis and Mountain Backdrops

The urban areas of Las Vegas and Reno are masterfully woven with pockets of green spaces amidst the desert backdrop. Las Vegas's Springs Preserve and Reno's Rancho San Rafael Regional Park offer lush, serene escapes within their bustling confines. The surrounding mountains provide a dramatic contrast to the city skylines and are a haven for hiking, biking, and skiing.

Central Basins and Ranges: The Heart of Nevada

Central Nevada is characterized by its dramatic basin and range topography, where long stretches of flat valleys are abruptly met by rugged mountain ranges. This region is dotted with hidden gems such as the historic town of Ely and the striking Lehman Caves at Great Basin National Park. The fall here transforms the high desert into a canvas of muted golds and browns, while the valleys and creeks provide a sanctuary for wildlife.

The Sierra Nevada: Majestic Mountains on the Western Edge

Western Nevada shares the majestic Sierra Nevada range with California. This area is a paradise for nature lovers and outdoor enthusiasts, with Lake Tahoe offering pristine waters and ski resorts that are among the best in the world. The region is also known for its arts and culture, epitomized by the Nevada Museum of Art in Reno and the historical treasures in Carson City. Mount Rose, the highest peak entirely within Nevada, offers spectacular views and challenging trails.

Mojave's Mystique: Southern Nevada's Desert and Resorts

No exploration of Nevada's landscape is complete without venturing into the iconic Mojave Desert. Home to Las Vegas, this region blends natural beauty with human-made wonders. The Red Rock Canyon National Conservation Area provides a stark, beautiful contrast to the neon lights of the Strip, while the Lake Mead National Recreation Area offers water-based activities in one of the harshest desert climates.

Rivers and Lakes: Lifelines of the Desert

Nevada is also a state of striking contrasts where rivers and lakes form vital oases. The Colorado River, forming Nevada's southeastern border, creates recreational havens at Lake Mead and Laughlin. The Truckee River provides both a water source and recreational heartline flowing from Lake Tahoe through Reno.

In Conclusion

The landscapes of Nevada are as dramatic and diverse as its cities and cultural history. From the serene deserts to the snowy mountain peaks, from glittering urban landscapes to tranquil waterways, Nevada's natural beauty offers a rich tapestry that enchants every traveler. As you journey through these landscapes, remember that they are not just a backdrop but an integral part of the story of Nevada.

The Flora and Fauna of Nevada

In *Nevada Travel Guide*, we not only explore vibrant cities and historic sites but also delve into the rich tapestry of natural life that Nevada harbors. This chapter is dedicated to exploring the diverse flora and fauna that enrich the landscapes of the Silver State, offering a glimpse into the vibrant ecosystems that thrive in this unique environment.

Flora: A Botanical Mosaic

Nevada's flora is a vibrant mosaic, shaped by its varied geography, from arid desert basins to mountainous regions. Each area boasts its own unique plant life that has adapted to the extreme conditions.

Desert Vegetation: In the Mojave and Great Basin deserts, hardy, drought-resistant plants dominate. Creosote bush, Joshua tree, sagebrush, and various cacti species are prevalent, each uniquely adapted to the dry climate.

Mountain Flora: Higher elevations like the Sierra Nevada and the Spring Mountains support coniferous forests. Here, pinyon pine, juniper, and mountain mahogany are common, providing a stark contrast to the desert below.

Riparian Areas: Along rivers and lakes, lush riparian habitats thrive. Cottonwoods, willows, and wildflowers line the waterways, creating vital ecosystems in the arid landscape.

Unique Species: Nevada is home to unique plant species such as the ancient bristlecone pine, one of the oldest living organisms on Earth, found in the higher mountains. The state flower, sagebrush, is widespread across the desert plains.

Fauna: From Deserts to Mountains

The animal life in Nevada is as diverse as its flora, ranging from desert dwellers to mountain inhabitants.

Desert Wildlife: The deserts of Nevada are home to a variety of animals adapted to the harsh environment. Bighorn sheep, desert tortoises, and coyotes roam the landscape, while Gila monsters and various lizard species bask in the sun.

Mountain Fauna: In the cooler, forested mountain regions, wildlife includes mule deer, mountain lions, and elk. The higher altitude and dense forests provide a starkly different habitat from the desert below.

Birds: Nevada is a key location for birdwatching, especially during migrations. Lakes such as the Lahontan Reservoir attract waterfowl, while raptors like the golden eagle and red-tailed hawk are commonly seen soaring above the mountains and valleys.

Insects and Reptiles: Insects, including the vividly colored butterflies and various bee species, play vital roles in pollination. Reptiles, notably rattlesnakes, thrive in Nevada's varied habitats, adapted perfectly to the regional challenges.

Preservation and Conservation Efforts

Nevada is committed to preserving its natural heritage. State parks, national forests, and protected areas like the Ash Meadows National Wildlife Refuge ensure the survival of many species and their habitats. Conservation efforts, including water resource management and protection of endangered species like the Lahontan cutthroat trout, highlight the state's dedication to its natural environment.

In Conclusion

The flora and fauna of Nevada are integral to the state's identity and allure. They add depth and complexity to the landscape and are essential for ecological balance. As you explore the destinations in this guide, take a moment to appreciate the natural beauty and biodiversity that Nevada has to offer. It's not just about the places we visit, but also about the living tapestry that forms the backdrop of our journey.

The Climate of Nevada

In *Nevada Travel Guide*, the climate plays a crucial role in shaping the experiences of each destination. This chapter explores the climate of Nevada, offering insights into how it influences the landscapes, flora, fauna, and the overall travel experience across the state.

Seasonal Variations: A Year-Round Perspective

Nevada experiences a mostly arid desert climate, with significant variations between day and night and across different regions of the state. The state's climate brings its own unique charm and challenges throughout the year.

Spring (March to May): This season sees a gradual warming, with temperatures still cool, particularly in the mornings and evenings. The desert blooms with wildflowers, particularly after wet winters, offering spectacular displays.

Summer (June to August): Summers in Nevada are hot and dry, especially in regions like Las Vegas and the Mojave Desert. High temperatures often exceed 100°F. However, the northern and higher altitude areas, like Reno and the Sierra Nevada, can be more temperate.

Fall (September to November): Fall brings cooler temperatures and is an excellent time for outdoor activities such as hiking and wildlife viewing. The weather remains pleasant, with warm days and crisp nights, ideal for exploring both urban and natural settings.

Winter (December to February): Winters can be quite cold, especially in the northern and higher altitude areas, where snow is common and offers opportunities for winter sports such as skiing and snowboarding. Southern Nevada experiences milder winters, making it a popular destination for those seeking to escape colder climates.

Regional Climate Differences

The climate in Nevada varies significantly from region to region:

Southern Nevada: This area, including Las Vegas, experiences very hot summers and mild winters, making it a year-round destination. The extreme heat in summer encourages indoor activities or visiting higher altitude areas nearby for cooler temperatures.

Northern Nevada: Regions such as Reno experience more pronounced seasonal changes with colder winters and milder summers than the southern part of the state. Snowfall is more common, providing opportunities for winter sports in the Sierra Nevada mountains.

Central and Eastern Nevada: These areas are characterized by more extreme temperature fluctuations between day and night and a more pronounced desert climate, with very hot summers and cold winters.

Impact of Climate Change

Climate change is noticeably impacting Nevada, with increased temperatures and changing precipitation patterns affecting water resources and wildlife habitats. This is particularly significant in desert areas and the Sierra Nevada, where snowpack variations influence water availability.

Preparing for Travel

When planning a visit to Nevada, consider the seasonal variations:

Spring and Summer: Lightweight, breathable clothing is essential for the daytime heat, along with a hat and sunscreen. However, nighttime in the desert can be cool, so a light jacket or sweater may be necessary.

Fall: Layered clothing works best as temperatures can vary significantly between day and night.

Winter: In the north and higher elevations, warm clothing and snow gear are essential for outdoor activities. In the south, lighter winter clothing will usually suffice.

In Conclusion

The climate of Nevada adds depth to the state's appeal, offering a dynamic backdrop that changes with the seasons. Whether you're exploring the vibrant nightlife of Las Vegas, hiking in the cool Sierra Nevada, or enjoying the stark beauty of the desert in bloom, understanding the climate will enhance your experience and help you prepare for a memorable visit.

The History of Nevada

In *Nevada Travel Guide,* the history of Nevada is explored as a crucial element of the state's identity. This chapter guides you through the rich historical narrative that has shaped Nevada into the diverse and dynamic state it is today.

Indigenous Roots and Colonial Beginnings

Long before European influence, Nevada was inhabited by Native American tribes such as the Washoe, Paiute, and Shoshone. Their deep connection with the land laid the foundational culture of the region.

The mid-19th century ushered in a wave of non-native explorers and settlers, spurred by the promise of wealth and new opportunities. Nevada gained considerable attention during the 1859 Comstock Lode discovery, which produced immense silver deposits, leading to a mining boom and ultimately to Nevada's statehood in 1864 during the Civil War.

Gateway to the West

Nevada's strategic location made it a critical point during westward expansion. The establishment of the Pony Express and the completion of the Transcontinental Railroad through Nevada in the 1860s facilitated faster movement of people and goods, profoundly shaping the state's development and integration into the broader United States.

The Rise of the Entertainment and Gaming Industry

The early 20th century marked a significant shift for Nevada as it embraced legalized gambling in 1931, setting the stage for its future as a premier entertainment destination. The construction of the Hoover Dam, completed in 1936, was a monumental project that significantly boosted Nevada's economy and population through the Great Depression.

Modern Era and Transformation

Throughout the 20th century, Nevada became synonymous with both leisure and innovation. Las Vegas, known globally for its vibrant nightlife and casinos, and Reno, "The Biggest Little City in the World," continued to evolve as centers for gambling and entertainment. Meanwhile, areas like Area 51 contributed to Nevada's mystique and association with advanced military and aerospace technology.

Cultural Melting Pot

Nevada's history is also marked by its transformation into a cultural melting pot, with significant contributions from diverse communities, including Hispanic and Asian populations, which have enriched the state's cultural landscape.

Historical Landmarks and Legacy

Nevada is scattered with historical landmarks that narrate its past. From the neon-lit streets of Las Vegas to the historic mining towns like Virginia City, and from the natural beauty of Lake Tahoe to the engineering marvel of the Hoover Dam, these sites provide a deep insight into Nevada's developmental saga.

In Conclusion

Understanding the history of Nevada is essential for appreciating its present. From its indigenous roots, through its pivotal role in the mining boom, to its current status as a global entertainment hub, Nevada's history is a testament to the adaptability and enduring spirit of its people. As you explore the destinations in this guide, take a moment to reflect on the historical significance of each location and how it has contributed to the diverse tapestry that is Nevada today.

Reno and Western Nevada

1.   Lake Tahoe

Lake Tahoe is not just a destination; it is a visual spectacle nestled between California and Nevada, boasting some of the most stunning landscapes in North America. As the largest alpine lake on the continent, Lake Tahoe captivates visitors with its panoramic vistas of crystal-clear waters set against the backdrop of towering mountain peaks. The lake's vast expanse covers about 191 square miles, with depths reaching up to 1,645 feet, making it the second deepest lake in the United States.

The natural beauty of Lake Tahoe has been a magnet for tourists year-round, offering a plethora of activities regardless of the season. During the warmer months, the lake is a hub for outdoor enthusiasts. Boating, kayaking, and paddleboarding are popular on the water, providing a unique perspective of the lake's vastness and the surrounding natural beauty. The sandy beaches and secluded coves around the lake offer ideal spots for relaxation and family picnics.

For adventurers, the surrounding Sierra Nevada Mountains offer endless hiking and biking trails. These paths wind through lush forests and over scenic ridges, offering breathtaking views of the lake below. In the winter, Lake Tahoe transforms into a premier ski destination, with several world-class ski resorts draped around its rim. These resorts become playgrounds for skiing, snowboarding, and other winter sports, attracting enthusiasts from around the globe.

The cultural vibe of Lake Tahoe is as diverse as its landscape. The lake's shores are dotted with quaint towns each offering unique dining and shopping experiences. Festivals and events throughout the year celebrate everything from local cuisine to international music, adding a rich layer of cultural experiences to the natural attractions.

Environmental conservation efforts are crucial to maintaining Lake Tahoe's pristine condition. Initiatives aimed at preserving water clarity and promoting sustainable tourism practices ensure that the natural beauty of the lake can be enjoyed for generations to come.

2. Sand Harbor

Sand Harbor, with its gently sloping beaches and crystalline waters, is one of Lake Tahoe's most scenic spots. Located on the northeastern shores of the lake within Nevada's Lake Tahoe Nevada State Park, this area is renowned for its stunning beauty and recreational opportunities. The harbor features expansive sandy beaches, clear waters, and dramatic rock formations, creating a picturesque setting perfect for photography and relaxation.

The clear waters of Sand Harbor make it an ideal spot for swimming, snorkeling, and scuba diving. Visibility can reach up to 70 feet on a clear day, revealing an underwater world of rock formations and aquatic life. Kayaking and paddleboarding are also popular, allowing visitors to explore the coastline at their own pace and venture to nearby hidden coves and beaches.

Sand Harbor is not just about water sports; it is also a cultural hub in the summer months. The Lake Tahoe Shakespeare Festival, hosted here, combines outstanding theatrical productions with the natural amphitheater provided by the surrounding landscape. Visitors can watch classic plays unfold in the open air, with Lake Tahoe providing a stunning backdrop.

Facilities at Sand Harbor include picnic areas equipped with tables and grills, making it a perfect spot for a family outing. The beaches are well-maintained with gentle slopes that offer safe swimming conditions for children and less experienced swimmers. The park also features several hiking trails that offer varied terrain and panoramic views of the lake.

The commitment to maintaining the natural beauty of Sand Harbor is evident in the carefully managed visitor capacities and conservation efforts. These initiatives help preserve the area's pristine condition and ensure that it remains a cherished destination for future visitors.

3.   Washoe Lake State Park

Located in the scenic Washoe Valley between Reno and Carson City, Nevada, Washoe Lake State Park offers a striking contrast to the alpine setting of nearby Lake Tahoe. This park features a blend of high desert landscape and expansive wetlands, providing a unique backdrop for a variety of recreational activities.

Washoe Lake, the centerpiece of the park, is known for its fluctuating water levels, which can dramatically change the landscape from season to season. The lake is a favorite among local windsurfers and sailors who take advantage of the strong winds that are common in the valley. The surrounding wetlands attract a diverse array of wildlife, making the park a popular spot for birdwatching and nature photography.

The park offers numerous trails for hiking, horseback riding, and mountain biking, which provide fantastic views of the Sierra Nevada and the Virginia Range. These trails range from easy walks along the lake's edge to more challenging hikes up the surrounding hills. The diverse terrain allows visitors to experience the beauty of the Nevada high desert, with its unique flora and fauna.

Camping facilities at Washoe Lake State Park include sites with hook-ups for RVs as well as tent camping spots, offering a range of options for overnight stays. Each site provides a base to enjoy the tranquility of the park under a canopy of stars, often clear enough to spot constellations and other celestial sights.

The park's commitment to preserving its natural environment is evident in its well-maintained trails and informative visitor center, which offers educational programs about the local ecosystem and history. Washoe Lake State Park serves not only as a recreational area but also as an important habitat for wildlife and a place for visitors to connect with nature away from the busier tourist spots.

4.   Mt. Rose Ski Tahoe

Located just a short drive from the shores of Lake Tahoe, Mt. Rose Ski Tahoe offers some of the most accessible high-altitude skiing in the Tahoe region. With a base elevation of 8,260 feet, it is the highest base of any Tahoe ski resort, providing a longer skiing season and often better snow conditions.

Mt. Rose Ski Tahoe is known for its varied terrain, catering to all skill levels from beginners to advanced skiers. The resort features over 1,200 acres of skiable terrain with more than 60 trails and several challenging chutes in The Chutes area, which offers some of the steepest inbounds skiing in North America. For beginners, the resort has gentle slopes and wide runs that are perfect for learning and improving skiing or snowboarding skills.

The resort's location provides spectacular views of both Lake Tahoe and the surrounding Nevada desert, making it a unique spot for skiing and snowboarding. The proximity to Reno also makes Mt. Rose a popular choice for visitors who want to combine a ski trip with some urban entertainment.

Mt. Rose Ski Tahoe is not just about winter sports; it also offers summer activities such as hiking and mountain biking, utilizing the ski lifts for easy access to high-altitude trails. This makes it a year-round destination for outdoor enthusiasts.

The resort is committed to providing a great skiing experience with high-quality facilities, including modern lifts, a cozy lodge, and a range of dining options. With its family-friendly atmosphere, excellent snow conditions, and convenient location, Mt. Rose Ski Tahoe continues to be a favorite among Tahoe skiers and snowboarders.

5.   Galena Creek Park

Nestled in the scenic foothills of the Sierra Nevada, Galena Creek Park is a natural oasis offering an escape into the beauty of northern Nevada's diverse landscapes. The park, spread across several thousand acres, is located between Reno and Lake Tahoe and serves as a prime spot for outdoor activities and environmental education. The park's terrain varies from gentle creekside paths to rugged mountain trails, providing opportunities for visitors of all fitness levels to explore the area's natural beauty.

Galena Creek Park is renowned for its rich biodiversity, which includes towering Jeffrey pines, lush aspen groves, and a vibrant array of wildflowers during the spring and summer months. Wildlife is abundant, with chances to spot deer, coyotes, and a variety of bird species, including the occasional bald eagle. The park's ecosystem is a focal point of the visitor center's educational programs, which offer guided hikes, nature talks, and interactive displays for children and adults alike.

The park features several well-marked trails that cater to both casual walkers and serious hikers. The Jones Creek Trail is particularly popular for its moderate challenge and the stunning views it offers of the surrounding mountains. For those interested in winter sports, the park's higher elevations provide excellent opportunities for cross-country skiing and snowshoeing in the snowy months.

Recreational facilities at Galena Creek Park include picnic areas equipped with tables and grills, making it a perfect destination for family outings. The park also hosts various events throughout the year, including music concerts in the outdoor amphitheater, star-gazing nights, and seasonal festivals that celebrate the natural environment and local culture.

Environmental conservation is a key focus for the park's management, with ongoing efforts to preserve the natural habitats and maintain the trails. These efforts ensure that Galena Creek Park remains a welcoming and sustainable space for future visitors to enjoy the tranquility and natural beauty of the Sierra Nevada foothills.

6.   Historic Fourth Ward School Museum

The Historic Fourth Ward School Museum stands as a remarkable testament to the educational practices of the late 19th century in the American West. Located in Virginia City, Nevada, this architectural gem is the last standing four-story wooden school building in America. Built in 1876 during the height of the Comstock Lode mining boom, the school offered education to the children of miners and businessmen flocking to the area in search of fortune.

Today, the museum offers visitors a glimpse into the past, with classrooms preserved exactly as they were when the school was operational. Each classroom serves as a mini-exhibit, displaying period furniture, textbooks, and educational materials from the 19th century. The museum also explores the broader history of Virginia City, providing insights into the daily lives of its residents during the mining boom.

One of the highlights of the museum is its extensive archival collection, which includes original photographs, documents, and personal items belonging to former students and teachers. These artifacts offer a poignant glimpse into the personal histories of those who lived through one of the most exciting and tumultuous periods in Nevada's history.

The Historic Fourth Ward School Museum is more than just a building; it's an educational resource that offers year-round programming, including lectures, workshops, and special events aimed at preserving and sharing the rich history of Virginia City. Its continued operation serves as a cultural anchor in the community, educating future generations about the importance of history and preservation.

7.   Virginia City Historic District

Virginia City Historic District transports visitors back to the boom days of the 19th-century mining era. As the site of the Comstock Lode, which triggered the silver rush of 1859, this town boasts a rich history encapsulated within its preserved buildings and cobbled streets. Today, it stands as a meticulously maintained historic district, offering a rare, immersive experience into the mining culture that once dominated the American West.

Walking through the district, visitors can explore an array of authentic saloons, museums, and shops that line the wooden sidewalks. The town's architecture is a mix of Victorian buildings and rustic wooden structures that house everything from antique stores to modern eateries, creating a vibrant contrast between the old and the new.

Key attractions include the Virginia and Truckee Railroad, which offers scenic rides around the area, providing breathtaking views of the rugged Nevada landscape. The Mark Twain Museum, situated in the building where Samuel Clemens first used his famous pen name, delves into the life and times of the iconic American writer during his early years as a reporter in Virginia City.

The town is not just a static museum piece; it is a living community that celebrates its heritage with numerous events throughout the year, such as the celebrated Camel and Ostrich Races, which humorously commemorate the quirky history of mining towns using animals for transport and entertainment. The Virginia City Historic District is an essential destination for those seeking to understand the historical significance and enduring legacy of the mining era in Nevada.

8.   Fort Churchill State Historic Park

Fort Churchill State Historic Park, located along the Carson River in Nevada, offers a unique blend of history and natural beauty. Established in 1861 to protect early settlers and maintain order in the region, the fort's ruins have been preserved as a reminder of Nevada's early military history. The park not only serves as a historical site but also provides a serene natural environment for a variety of outdoor activities.

Visitors to the park can explore the remains of the fort, where informative plaques detail its history and the daily lives of soldiers stationed here. The visitor center offers additional insights with exhibits on the fort's construction, its role in the Paiute War, and its later use as a waystation for travelers on the Pony Express.

The surrounding area is a haven for wildlife enthusiasts and outdoor adventurers. The park's network of trails invites hikers, bikers, and equestrians to explore the scenic beauty of the Nevada landscape, which includes lush riverine habitats and expansive desert vistas. Birdwatchers are particularly drawn to the park, as it is home to a diverse array of bird species that thrive along the river corridor.

Camping facilities at Fort Churchill are well-equipped, providing visitors with the opportunity to stay overnight and enjoy the peaceful, starlit nights typical of the Nevada desert. The park also hosts various educational programs and living history events, allowing visitors to experience military drills and life as it was during the fort's operational years.

Fort Churchill State Historic Park serves as a poignant reminder of Nevada's military past while offering a peaceful retreat for nature lovers and history enthusiasts alike, making it a comprehensive and enriching destination for all visitors.

9. Crystal Peak Park

Crystal Peak Park, nestled in the picturesque landscape of Verdi, Nevada, near the California border, offers a serene escape into nature's embrace. Originally the site of a logging and ice harvesting operation in the late 1800s, the park today is a harmonious blend of historical significance and natural beauty. Spanning approximately 56 acres, it provides a peaceful retreat with its lush meadows, dense groves of pine trees, and the gentle waters of the Truckee River flowing through it.

The park's namesake, Crystal Peak, refers to the glittering quartz crystals once abundant in the area, which drew prospectors and miners during the 19th century. Today, visitors might still find small remnants of quartz in the area, a nod to the park's sparkling past. This historic context adds a layer of intrigue and exploration for those visiting the park, making it not just a natural getaway but also a journey through the local history.

Crystal Peak Park is ideally suited for family outings and nature enthusiasts alike. The well-maintained picnic areas, complete with tables and barbecue grills, make it a favorite spot for group gatherings and family picnics. Children can enjoy the playground, while adults appreciate the horseshoe pits and volleyball courts, offering leisure and recreational activities for all ages.

The park also features several walking trails that meander through the forest and along the river. These trails are perfect for a peaceful stroll, a brisk hike, or even mountain biking, providing different ways to appreciate the scenic views and perhaps catch a glimpse of local wildlife. Birdwatchers will find the park a haven for observing a variety of bird species, particularly during the migration seasons.

Fishing enthusiasts are drawn to the waters of the Truckee River within the park, known for its excellent trout fishing. The river's accessibility allows for both fly fishing and conventional angling, making it a popular destination for both novice and experienced anglers.

Crystal Peak Park also serves as a venue for community events, including weddings, family reunions, and local festivals. Its natural beauty provides a picturesque backdrop for photography, and the tranquil setting is ideal for those special occasions.

10.   Nevada Museum of Art

Located in the heart of Reno, the Nevada Museum of Art stands as a cultural beacon in the state, dedicated to the exploration of the visual arts with a distinctive focus on the environment. Founded in 1931, it is the oldest cultural institution in Nevada and has grown to become a leader in the arts community, both regionally and nationally. The museum's building, designed by architect Will Bruder, is a work of art in itself, featuring a unique design inspired by the geological formations of the Black Rock Desert and the Sierra Nevada mountains.

The museum's permanent collection includes over 2,000 works of art with a strong emphasis on contemporary and historical artworks that explore the interactions between humans and their environments. This thematic focus is part of the museum's mission to engage people in the appreciation of art that reflects and shapes our understanding of the world. The collection features works from a range of mediums, including painting, photography, sculpture, and mixed media, by both renowned and emerging artists.

Exhibitions at the Nevada Museum of Art are thoughtfully curated to provide insights into diverse artistic perspectives and to stimulate discussion among visitors. These exhibitions often address topical issues such as sustainability, conservation, and cultural heritage, reflecting the museum's commitment to fostering a community that is knowledgeable about the arts and aware of global and environmental issues.

The museum also houses the Center for Art + Environment, an internationally recognized research center that archives, exhibits, and fosters creative work at the intersection of the arts and the environment. This center has a vast archive that includes artists' sketches, journals, and other materials that document the creative process in engaging with environmental themes.

Educational programs at the Nevada Museum of Art are extensive, ranging from workshops and lectures to tours and art classes for all ages. The museum's efforts to educate and involve the community extend beyond its walls through outreach programs that bring art education to schools and community centers across the region.

11.   Truckee River Walk

The Truckee River Walk in Reno, Nevada, is a vibrant and picturesque pathway that follows the course of the Truckee River through the heart of the city. This delightful promenade has transformed the riverfront into a lively hub of activity, drawing both locals and tourists to enjoy its scenic beauty and the plethora of activities it offers.

Spanning several miles, the River Walk provides a peaceful setting for walking, jogging, and cycling, with beautifully landscaped parks, benches, and viewing platforms along the way. It starts from the downtown area, where the river's presence adds a refreshing touch to the urban environment, and extends to the more tranquil spaces where the natural beauty of the Truckee River can be fully appreciated.

Along the River Walk, visitors can explore a variety of shops, restaurants, and cafes that offer everything from fine dining to casual eats, with many places featuring outdoor seating that overlooks the river. This setup not only enhances the dining experience but also contributes to the lively atmosphere of the River Walk, making it a perfect spot for a leisurely afternoon or an evening out.

Cultural attractions are abundant along the River Walk. Art installations, sculptures, and murals add an artistic flair to the area, celebrating local artists and the cultural heritage of Reno. Seasonal events and festivals hosted along the River Walk, such as wine walks, art festivals, and live music performances, provide entertainment and fun for all ages, contributing to the community's vibrant social scene.

For those interested in history and nature, the River Walk includes access to several parks and historic sites along its route. These areas offer educational displays about the ecology of the Truckee River and the history of Reno, providing a deeper understanding and appreciation of the area.

12.   National Automobile Museum

The National Automobile Museum in Reno, Nevada, is a must-visit destination for car enthusiasts and history buffs alike. Regarded as one of the finest automobile museums in the world, it houses a collection of more than 200 cars that chronicle the history of automobile innovation and design. The museum is a legacy of casino magnate Bill Harrah, whose original collection formed the basis of what visitors see today.

Upon entering the museum, visitors are transported through time, beginning with the late 19th century and progressing to modern-day automotive marvels. The collection includes everything from horseless carriages and classic luxury vehicles to muscle cars and race cars, each with its own story and significance. Notable highlights include the Thomas Flyer, winner of the 1908 New York to Paris automobile race, and Elvis Presley's 1973 Cadillac Eldorado.

The museum's displays are arranged in street scenes that recreate the historical context in which these vehicles were driven. These vignettes include facades of old buildings, street lamps, and artifacts that add to the immersive experience, allowing visitors to visualize the era in which these cars roamed the streets.

Educational programs at the National Automobile Museum are designed to engage visitors of all ages, with workshops, guided tours, and interactive exhibits that explain the technological advances and cultural impacts of the automotive industry. The museum also hosts special events, including car shows and automotive lectures that delve deeper into the fascinations with car culture.

For those with a passion for automotive history, or for families looking for an engaging educational experience, the National Automobile Museum offers a comprehensive and captivating look at how automobiles have shaped our social and cultural landscape.

13.   Reno Arch

The Reno Arch is an iconic symbol of Reno, Nevada, often referred to as "The Biggest Little City in the World." Standing proudly at the intersection of Virginia Street and Commercial Row, this distinctive landmark embodies the vibrant and spirited character of Reno. Originally erected in 1926 to promote the Nevada Transcontinental Highway Exposition, the arch has undergone several transformations and relocations, each reflecting changes in the city's image and ambitions.

Today's arch, the third iteration, features brilliant neon lights and a glowing emblematic slogan that captures the essence of Reno's identity. Its current design was selected through a public contest in 1987, emphasizing modernity while preserving the nostalgic charm of its predecessors. At night, the illuminated arch provides a striking visual against the backdrop of downtown Reno, offering a popular photo opportunity for visitors and a beloved backdrop for various city events.

The Reno Arch isn't just a visual landmark; it serves as a cultural and historical touchstone for the city. It has witnessed nearly a century of Reno's evolution, from a small railway town to a bustling hub for entertainment and gambling. The arch has been a silent observer to the many phases of economic booms and downturns, adapting and enduring as a steadfast symbol of local pride.

Visitors to the arch can explore the surrounding area, which is rich in entertainment and historical sites. Nearby, the vibrant Riverwalk District offers an array of shops, restaurants, and galleries, while several casinos provide insight into the gambling heritage that shaped much of Reno's development. The arch's central location also makes it an ideal starting point for city tours and a focal point during special events like the Reno River Festival and Hot August Nights, a classic car convention that transforms the city into a nostalgic celebration of mid-20th-century Americana.

As a piece of public art and historical artifact, the Reno Arch goes beyond its role as a mere architectural feature. It is a beacon of local culture, welcoming visitors and residents alike to explore and appreciate the lively community and rich history of Reno.

14. Sparks Marina Park

Sparks Marina Park in Sparks, Nevada, is a testament to innovative urban redevelopment. What was once an operational gravel pit was transformed into a thriving recreational and residential hub. Covering over 70 acres, the centerpiece of the park is a 77-acre man-made lake, created from the water-filled excavation site, which offers a multitude of water-based activities and a scenic oasis in the heart of the city.

The park's well-maintained surroundings feature walking and cycling trails that loop around the lake, providing perfect paths for leisurely strolls or vigorous runs. These trails are not only practical but also offer stunning views of the water and the surrounding Sierra Nevada mountains, creating a tranquil environment for relaxation and physical activity.

Water sports enthusiasts find Sparks Marina Park particularly appealing. The lake is zoned for swimming, fishing, boating, and even scuba diving, with a designated beach area that includes a swimming cove, safeguarded by lifeguards during peak summer months. The clear waters and managed fish populations make for excellent fishing conditions, while the presence of diverse marine life appeals to adventurous scuba divers.

Beyond water activities, the park is equipped with picnic areas, volleyball courts, and playgrounds, making it an ideal location for family gatherings and community events. The park also includes a dog park, ensuring that every family member, including four-legged ones, can enjoy a day out. During the year, the park hosts several events and festivals, further enhancing its role as a community focal point.

Sparks Marina Park stands as a successful example of how urban spaces can be beautifully reclaimed and repurposed. It provides a multifunctional urban green space that caters to a wide range of interests and activities, promoting an active and engaged community life. Whether one is seeking adventure on the water, a peaceful afternoon in nature, or a vibrant community event, Sparks Marina Park offers something for everyone, making it a cherished destination within the city of Sparks.

15.   Fleischmann Planetarium

Located on the campus of the University of Nevada, Reno, Fleischmann Planetarium is a gateway to the stars, offering visitors a chance to explore the cosmos through high-quality exhibits, educational programs, and one of the first dome theaters in the world. Since its inception in 1963, the planetarium has been dedicated to expanding public understanding of the universe while providing an engaging learning environment for all ages.

The building itself, designed by renowned architect Raymond M. Hellmann, is a striking example of Mid-Century Modern architecture. Its unique hyperbolic paraboloid structure is not only aesthetically significant but also functionally enhances the acoustics and visual experience inside the dome theater. This theater hosts a variety of immersive shows that transport audiences across the solar system, through distant galaxies, and into the depths of the universe, all from the comfort of their seats.

Fleischmann Planetarium's exhibitions are designed to educate and inspire. They include interactive displays that explain complex astronomical concepts in accessible ways, models of spacecraft, and artifacts related to space exploration. Special exhibits often feature topics like black holes, the search for extraterrestrial life, and the latest advancements in astronomy.

Educational outreach is a cornerstone of the planetarium's mission. It offers a range of programs designed to spark interest in science, technology, engineering, and math (STEM) fields. These programs include school field trips, family science nights, and telescope viewing parties, where visitors can observe celestial events and phenomena through high-powered telescopes, guided by knowledgeable staff.

For those fascinated by the stars, or families looking for an educational outing, Fleischmann Planetarium is a resource-rich destination. It not only provides insights into the universe but also encourages a deeper appreciation for the wonders of science and the vastness of space.

16. Rancho San Rafael Regional Park

Rancho San Rafael Regional Park is a comprehensive outdoor recreation area in Reno, Nevada, that caters to a wide array of interests and activities. Covering over 600 acres, it encompasses everything from expansive green fields and serene ponds to rugged mountain terrain, offering numerous amenities and attractions within its boundaries.

The park is renowned for its diverse landscapes, which include manicured lawns, natural meadows, wetlands, and sagebrush hills. These varied environments provide habitats for many species of wildlife, making the park a haven for nature lovers and wildlife enthusiasts. The extensive network of trails invites visitors to hike, bike, or simply stroll, enjoying the natural beauty and tranquility of the area.

One of the park's highlights is the Wilbur D. May Center, a museum and botanical garden that showcases an impressive collection of artifacts and exhibits related to world travels and cultures, as well as lush gardens that display both native and exotic plants. The center also offers educational programs and cultural events that enhance visitors' understanding and appreciation of natural and cultural diversity.

For families, Rancho San Rafael Regional Park is equipped with playgrounds, picnic areas, and open spaces perfect for kite flying, frisbee, or a casual game of soccer. The park also features a dog park where pets can run and play off-leash in a safe and enclosed environment.

Throughout the year, the park serves as a venue for major community events, including the Great Reno Balloon Race, one of the largest free hot-air ballooning events in the world. This event fills the skies above the park with colorful balloons, providing a spectacular sight and drawing thousands of visitors from across the region.

Rancho San Rafael Regional Park is not just a place to visit; it is a community hub that offers a multitude of recreational and educational opportunities, making it a cherished asset for the residents of Reno and its visitors. Whether one is seeking a peaceful retreat into nature, a cultural experience, or active recreation, Rancho San Rafael Regional Park delivers with its vast offerings and welcoming atmosphere.

17. Sierra Safari Zoo

Sierra Safari Zoo, nestled in the scenic outskirts of Reno, Nevada, is northern Nevada's largest zoo. Established in 1989, it has grown from a modest collection of exotic animals into a cherished educational and conservation center.

The zoo houses over two hundred animals representing more than forty different species, including both exotic and endangered animals. Residents include lemurs, lions, tigers, and a range of primates, each living in habitats designed to closely mimic their natural environments. The zoo's commitment to animal welfare and education is evident in its well-maintained enclosures and informative signs about the animals' habitats, behaviors, and conservation status.

A key feature of Sierra Safari Zoo is its emphasis on interactive experiences. The zoo offers hands-on encounters, allowing visitors to feed and interact with some animals under the supervision of trained staff. These experiences are both thrilling and educational, fostering a deeper connection between people and the animals.

The zoo is noted for its successful breeding programs for endangered species, playing a critical role in global efforts to preserve biodiversity. These programs often collaborate with other zoos and conservation organizations, sharing knowledge and resources to enhance the survival prospects of these species.

Sierra Safari Zoo also provides a variety of educational programs for all ages, including guided tours, zookeeper talks, and special event days. These programs engage children and families in fun, informative activities. The zoo's educational outreach extends into the community, teaching local schoolchildren about wildlife conservation and environmental stewardship.

For those looking to support the zoo, Sierra Safari offers membership options that provide free admission for a year, discounts at the gift shop, and invitations to special members-only events. These memberships are crucial in funding the care of the animals and the zoo's conservation initiatives.

18. Animal Ark

Located in the high desert north of Reno, Nevada, Animal Ark is a wildlife sanctuary and educational center dedicated to inspiring environmental stewardship through wildlife conservation. Founded in 1981, Animal Ark occupies approximately 38 acres of naturally landscaped enclosures designed to provide permanent homes for mostly non-releasable wildlife. The sanctuary specializes in housing predators and other animals that, due to injury or imprinting, cannot survive in their natural habitat.

Animal Ark focuses heavily on education and conservation, offering a variety of programs that teach visitors about the importance of biodiversity and the role of predators within ecosystems. The sanctuary is home to a diverse range of species, including North American predators like bears, wolves, and mountain lions, as well as more exotic species such as cheetahs and jaguars. Each animal's enclosure is tailored to mimic their natural habitat as closely as possible and provide them with a safe, stress-free environment.

One of the most exciting features of Animal Ark is its cheetah conservation program. The sanctuary participates in efforts to raise awareness about cheetah conservation and has facilities specifically designed for the fast-moving cats. This includes a large run where the cheetahs can reach their top speed, offering a rare and thrilling spectacle for visitors. These cheetah runs are not only educational but also serve to keep the animals healthy and engaged.

Animal Ark offers a range of interactive educational programs aimed at both children and adults. These include wildlife presentations, feeding demonstrations, and special events throughout the year that allow visitors to learn about wildlife conservation in an interactive setting. The staff are passionate about their roles as educators and caretakers, making every visit informative and engaging.

As a non-profit organization, Animal Ark relies on admissions, memberships, donations, and volunteer support to maintain its operations and care for its residents. Its commitment to providing a sanctuary for animals in need and educating the public about wildlife conservation makes it an important institution in the Reno community and a valuable resource for conservation efforts globally.

19.   Pyramid Lake

Pyramid Lake, located 40 miles northeast of Reno, Nevada, is one of the largest natural lakes in the state of Nevada and an important remnant of the ancient Lake Lahontan that once covered much of the region during the last ice age. The lake is named for its distinctive pyramid-shaped rock formations along the shores, and it holds cultural, environmental, and recreational significance, particularly for the Paiute Tribe who manage the lake and surrounding reservations.

The lake's stark, otherworldly beauty and its deep blue waters are a draw for photographers and nature enthusiasts alike. As a terminal lake, Pyramid Lake has no outlet, with water leaving only by evaporation, leading to high levels of salts and minerals. These unique conditions create a habitat for the endangered cui-ui fish and the famous Lahontan cutthroat trout, a species that draws anglers from all over the world hoping to catch a trophy-sized fish.

Pyramid Lake is not just a fishing paradise; it offers a range of recreational activities. Kayaking, canoeing, and boating are popular on the lake, providing a peaceful experience on its vast, open waters. The surrounding landscape, characterized by high desert plains and rugged mountains, offers opportunities for hiking and wildlife viewing, particularly during the cooler months of the year.

Culturally, Pyramid Lake is a sacred site for the Paiute Tribe, who have inhabited the area for thousands of years. The lake features in many of their myths and legends and is a central part of their community and spirituality today. The tribe operates a museum near the lake, which offers insights into the Paiute culture and history, as well as the natural history of the lake itself.

Pyramid Lake also hosts several events throughout the year, including fishing tournaments and the famous Pyramid Lake Paiute Tribe's cultural celebration. These events are opportunities for visitors to engage with the local community and learn more about the area's unique cultural heritage.

Elko and Northern Nevada

1.   Ruby Lake National Wildlife Refuge

Ruby Lake National Wildlife Refuge, located in the high desert of northeastern Nevada, spans over 37,632 acres and is a critical habitat for numerous bird species and wildlife. Established in 1938 to provide sanctuary for migratory birds, it is a vital stopover for thousands of waterfowl and other migratory species traveling along the Pacific Flyway.

The refuge's heart is a large marsh system fed by the Franklin Lake Basin, featuring open water, bulrushes, cattails, and expansive meadows. This diverse ecosystem thrives with wildlife, making it a picturesque destination for those seeking solitude and a deep connection with nature.

Birdwatching is a primary activity at Ruby Lake, especially during the spring and fall migrations. Species such as the canvasback, Northern pintail, and sandhill cranes are frequent visitors, while the refuge is home to a significant population of the rare and elusive canvasback ducks during winter months.

Fishing is another popular pursuit, with excellent conditions for catching largemouth bass, rainbow trout, and other freshwater species. The marshes and canals offer anglers both challenge and reward amidst striking natural beauty.

Visitors can explore the refuge's landscapes and wildlife through a range of trails and viewing platforms. Hiking and photography are encouraged, with several trails winding through diverse habitats that provide close encounters with the area's flora and fauna. In winter, the refuge transforms into a snowy wonderland, ideal for cross-country skiing and snowshoeing.

Ruby Lake National Wildlife Refuge is committed to conservation and education, hosting programs and guided tours that focus on the importance of wetlands, wildlife conservation, and the role of refuges in preserving biological diversity.

2.   Humboldt National Forest

Spanning an impressive area of over 2.3 million acres in northeastern Nevada, Humboldt National Forest is one of the largest and most diverse national forests in the United States. The forest encompasses a vast range of landscapes, from high desert plains to rugged mountains, providing a refuge for a wide array of wildlife and plant species. This extensive area offers endless opportunities for recreation and exploration, making it a premier destination for adventurers and nature enthusiasts.

The diversity of Humboldt National Forest is perhaps its most striking feature. The forest includes prominent features such as the Ruby Mountains and East Humboldt Range, which are renowned for their breathtaking beauty and challenging terrain. The elevation within the forest varies dramatically, creating a mosaic of ecosystems from sagebrush-covered valleys to alpine forests and meadows.

Hiking and camping are among the most popular activities in Humboldt National Forest. With hundreds of miles of trails, including portions of the famous Ruby Crest Trail, hikers can explore scenic vistas, serene lakes, and diverse habitats. These trails range from easy walks through pine forests to strenuous hikes up rugged peaks, offering something for every skill level.

Winter transforms the landscape of Humboldt National Forest into a snowy paradise, ideal for skiing, snowboarding, and snowmobiling. The higher elevations receive abundant snowfall, providing excellent conditions for winter sports enthusiasts. The forest also offers designated areas for snowmobiling, making it a favorite destination for those seeking thrilling winter adventures.

For those interested in wildlife, Humboldt National Forest is home to an impressive variety of animals, including deer, mountain lions, and numerous bird species. The forest's vast areas of undisturbed land make it an excellent place for wildlife viewing and photography, offering chances to observe these animals in their natural habitats.

3.   Ruby Mountains

The Ruby Mountains are one of Nevada's most treasured landscapes, often referred to as the "Alps of Nevada" due to their stunning beauty and dramatic peaks. Located in northeastern Nevada, this mountain range spans approximately 90 miles and is known for its rugged cliffs, pristine alpine lakes, and diverse ecosystems. The Ruby Mountains are a sanctuary for outdoor enthusiasts, offering a wealth of recreational activities set against a backdrop of breathtaking scenic vistas.

The range is most famous for the Ruby Crest Trail, a 38-mile long trail that runs along the spine of the mountains and provides hikers with unparalleled views of the surrounding valleys and peaks. This trail is a highlight for serious backpackers, offering challenging terrain and remote wilderness access. Along the way, hikers can find numerous alpine lakes, such as Lamoille Lake and Liberty Lake, which are perfect spots for rest and reflection.

Winter sports are a significant draw in the Ruby Mountains, with heli-skiing being a particularly unique offering. The high peaks and consistent snow conditions make for some of the best backcountry skiing in North America. For those who prefer self-propelled adventures, cross-country skiing and snowshoeing are also popular, with several trails providing safe and scenic routes through the snow-covered landscape.

Wildlife viewing is another rewarding activity in the Ruby Mountains. The area is home to a rich variety of wildlife, including mountain goats, bighorn sheep, and elk. Birdwatchers can also delight in spotting high-altitude bird species that make their home in the forests and meadows of the high Sierra.

Conservation is a key aspect of managing the Ruby Mountains, with efforts focused on preserving the natural beauty and ecological integrity of the area. This includes managing human impact on the environment and participating in research and restoration projects that help maintain the health of the forests, waterways, and wildlife populations.

4.   Lamoille Canyon

Lamoille Canyon, located in the heart of the Ruby Mountains in northeastern Nevada, is a stunning glacial canyon that serves as the gateway to some of the most spectacular landscapes in the region. Known as the largest valley in the Ruby Mountains, Lamoille Canyon offers visitors a dramatic display of towering cliffs, rushing streams, and lush meadows that burst with wildflowers in the spring and summer.

The canyon is accessible via a 12-mile scenic byway, which winds its way through the canyon floor, offering easy access to a variety of recreational activities and breathtaking views. Along the drive, numerous pullouts and picnic areas provide spots to enjoy the scenery and the tranquil sounds of the Lamoille Creek, which flows alongside the road.

Hiking is a popular activity in Lamoille Canyon, with trails ranging from easy walks to challenging mountain climbs. One of the most popular trails, the Lamoille Lake Trail, leads to a beautiful alpine lake set against the backdrop of craggy peaks, offering a perfect spot for photography, fishing, or simply enjoying the peace of the high Sierra.

For those more inclined to technical climbs, Lamoille Canyon offers access to the Ruby Crest Trail and other high-elevation paths that present more of a challenge. These trails offer stunning views and the chance to observe wildlife in their natural alpine habitats.

In winter, Lamoille Canyon transforms into a wonderland for snow sports. The area is popular for snowshoeing, cross-country skiing, and snowmobiling, with the snow-packed conditions providing excellent opportunities for winter recreation.

Lamoille Canyon is not only a hub for outdoor activities but also a center for environmental education and conservation. The U.S. Forest Service operates a visitor center at the entrance to the canyon, offering educational displays about the local flora, fauna, geology, and the history of the area. This center is a resource for both casual visitors and serious naturalists looking to deepen their understanding of the ecological and geological forces that have shaped this unique landscape.

5.   Spring Creek Horse Palace

Spring Creek Horse Palace, nestled in the picturesque landscapes of Spring Creek, Nevada, is a premier destination for equestrian enthusiasts and those looking to experience the rich cowboy culture of the American West. This facility is renowned for its comprehensive offerings that cater to both competitive riders and recreational horse lovers, making it a hub of horse-related activities in the region.

The Horse Palace boasts extensive facilities that include multiple arenas, both indoor and outdoor, designed to host a variety of equestrian events such as roping, barrel racing, and show jumping. These well-maintained arenas are equipped with high-quality footing materials to ensure the safety and performance of the horses and riders. This makes the Horse Palace a favored venue for regional and national equestrian competitions, attracting participants and spectators from across the country.

In addition to competitive events, Spring Creek Horse Palace offers numerous recreational riding opportunities. Guided trail rides are available, allowing visitors to explore the surrounding scenic landscapes on horseback. These rides cater to all skill levels, from beginners to experienced riders, providing a unique way to experience the natural beauty of Nevada's high desert and mountainous terrain.

Educational programs are a key component of the offerings at Spring Creek Horse Palace. The facility provides riding lessons and horse training programs taught by experienced equestrians. These programs focus on everything from basic horse care and riding techniques to advanced competition skills, catering to a diverse range of interests and abilities.

For those who are passionate about horse culture, the Horse Palace occasionally hosts clinics and workshops led by renowned trainers and industry professionals. These events offer insights into horse behavior, training techniques, and the latest trends in equestrian sports, providing valuable learning opportunities for the local equestrian community.

The Horse Palace is not just about horses and riding; it is a community center that brings together people with a shared passion for equestrian sports and Western heritage.

6.   South Fork State Recreation Area

South Fork State Recreation Area, sprawling over 2,200 acres and surrounding the South Fork Reservoir, is a gem in northeastern Nevada, known for its wide array of outdoor activities and its stunning natural scenery. Located just south of Elko, this recreation area draws visitors with its promise of adventure and relaxation in a picturesque setting.

The South Fork Reservoir, the centerpiece of the recreation area, covers approximately 1,650 acres and is a haven for anglers and water sports enthusiasts. The lake is stocked with several species of fish, including rainbow trout, brown trout, and largemouth bass, making it a popular destination for fishing year-round. Ice fishing is particularly popular in the winter months, providing a unique challenge for those brave enough to take on the colder temperatures.

Boating is another key attraction at South Fork, with the reservoir offering ample space for everything from kayaking and canoeing to motorboating. The clear waters of the lake are perfect for these activities, providing a tranquil escape on the water with spectacular views of the surrounding mountains and wildlife.

For those who prefer to stay on land, South Fork State Recreation Area offers more than just water-based activities. The area is crisscrossed with trails suitable for hiking, mountain biking, and horseback riding, offering visitors the chance to explore the diverse landscapes of the high desert. These trails wind through sagebrush, grasslands, and hills, offering panoramic views and opportunities to spot local wildlife, including mule deer, antelope, and a variety of bird species.

Camping is a popular activity at South Fork, with several campgrounds and dispersed camping areas providing perfect spots to set up a tent or park an RV. These camping sites offer basic amenities and provide a great way to experience the natural beauty of the area overnight, under the stars.

South Fork State Recreation Area also serves as an educational resource, with informational displays and occasional guided tours that teach visitors about the local ecology, wildlife, and conservation efforts.

7. California Trail Historic Interpretive Center

Located in Elko, Nevada, the California Trail Historic Interpretive Center offers a profound look into the pivotal journeys of emigrants who traveled the California Trail during the mid-19th century. This center presents a detailed and immersive portrayal of over 250,000 settlers who ventured westward, seeking new opportunities and a better life during the California Gold Rush and beyond.

The interpretive center is situated on a historic site along the original California Trail and features a variety of exhibits that bring the stories of these pioneers to life. Through interactive displays, multimedia presentations, and authentic artifacts, visitors can gain a deep understanding of what life was like on the trail. Exhibits cover topics such as daily life on the trail, the challenges faced by emigrants, and the impact of the journey on the country's expansion.

One of the center's standout features is its full-scale replicas of wagons and other period vehicles, which offer a tangible sense of the conditions endured by the emigrants. These replicas, along with detailed dioramas and life-sized figures, create an engaging and educational experience for visitors of all ages.

The California Trail Historic Interpretive Center also offers several trails that lead from the facility into the surrounding landscape. These trails are lined with interpretive signs that provide insights into the natural history and the specific challenges faced by travelers in this region, such as crossing rivers or navigating mountain passes. Walking these trails, visitors can step back in time and imagine the vast caravans of wagons that once passed through the area.

Educational programs at the center are designed to engage school groups, tourists, and history enthusiasts. These programs often include live demonstrations of pioneer skills, such as blacksmithing, cooking, and quilting, giving visitors a hands-on appreciation of 19th-century frontier life.

8. Elko Hot Springs

Elko Hot Springs, located near the bustling town of Elko in northeastern Nevada, offers a soothing retreat with its natural geothermal pools. Known for their therapeutic properties and serene settings, these hot springs have been a local favorite and a visitor attraction for decades. The springs are part of Nevada's rich geothermal landscape, which includes numerous hot springs scattered throughout the state.

The hot springs near Elko vary in size and accessibility, with some being developed into resorts and others remaining as more rustic, natural soaking areas. These natural pools provide a perfect way to relax after a day of exploring the rugged landscapes of northern Nevada. The mineral-rich waters are reputed to have health benefits, including stress relief and muscle relaxation, making them a popular destination for those seeking a natural wellness experience.

The most accessible of these is the commercial spa facility, which offers a controlled environment with amenities such as changing rooms, lounging areas, and sometimes even spa services. This facility makes the hot springs accessible year-round, offering a warm, soothing escape even in the winter months when the surrounding landscape is blanketed in snow.

For those seeking a more natural experience, several undeveloped hot springs can be found in the wilder areas around Elko. These require a bit of hiking and are best visited with an awareness of leave-no-trace principles to keep the environment pristine. Soaking in these natural pools, with views of the open landscape under the vast Nevada sky, offers a uniquely tranquil experience that connects visitors with the natural world in a profound way.

Visitors to Elko Hot Springs should be prepared with appropriate gear for the conditions, especially when visiting the less developed springs. It's also important to check local conditions and access rules, as some areas may be on private land or subject to seasonal closures to protect local wildlife.

Whether you choose the comfort of a developed spa or the rustic charm of a natural pool, Elko Hot Springs provides a memorable and rejuvenating experience.

9. Carlin Trend Mining Tours

Nestled in the heart of Nevada, the Carlin Trend is one of the most productive gold mining areas in the United States and a cornerstone of the global gold mining industry. The region, named after the nearby town of Carlin, is renowned for its rich deposits and has been a significant player in the mining sector since the deposits were first discovered in the 1960s. The Carlin Trend Mining Tours offer a unique opportunity to explore this vibrant part of Nevada's heritage and gain insight into modern mining operations.

These tours are not only educational but also highly engaging, providing a firsthand look at the scale and technology involved in gold mining today. Visitors have the chance to see massive open pits, sophisticated milling operations, and the environmental management practices that modern mining companies use to minimize their impact on the natural landscape. The experience is both awe-inspiring and enlightening, showcasing the complex processes from extraction to the production of gold bars.

The guided tours are typically led by knowledgeable guides who explain the geology of the Carlin Trend, the types of gold deposits found in the area, and the history of gold mining in Nevada. Participants learn about the exploration techniques and the cutting-edge technology used to locate and extract gold from ore, as well as the steps taken to reclaim and restore mining sites after operations conclude.

Safety is a paramount concern on these tours, with visitors equipped with necessary safety gear and briefed on safety protocols before venturing into active mining areas. This preparation ensures that tour participants can focus on learning and enjoying their experience without concerns.

In addition to the technical and educational aspects, the Carlin Trend Mining Tours often discuss the economic impact of mining on the local community and the broader Nevada economy. They provide a perspective on the job opportunities created by the mining sector and its contributions to local infrastructure and services.

10.　Western Folklife Center

The Western Folklife Center, located in the historic Pioneer Hotel in Elko, Nevada, is a cultural institution dedicated to preserving and presenting the arts, culture, and heritage of the American West. Through a variety of exhibitions, performances, and educational programs, the center plays a crucial role in keeping the spirit and traditions of the Western lifestyle alive and vibrant.

One of the center's flagship events is the annual National Cowboy Poetry Gathering, an internationally renowned festival that celebrates the skills, art forms, and stories of ranching and rural life. This event attracts poets, musicians, and artists from all over the world, providing them with a platform to share their talents and stories with enthusiastic audiences. The gathering is more than just an event; it is a community celebration that fosters a deeper understanding and appreciation of the cowboy culture and its significance to American heritage.

The Western Folklife Center also houses permanent and rotating exhibits that explore various aspects of Western life. These exhibits feature everything from handcrafted cowboy gear and Native American art to multimedia presentations that tell the stories of the men and women who live and work in the West. The exhibits are thoughtfully curated to provide insights into the historical and contemporary West, highlighting the diversity and complexity of its people and landscapes.

Educational programs at the Western Folklife Center are designed to engage participants of all ages. Workshops, demonstrations, and interactive sessions offer hands-on experiences in traditional Western arts such as leatherworking, silver smithing, and saddlery. These programs are led by experts and artisans who are passionate about their crafts and eager to share their knowledge with others.

The Western Folklife Center serves as a vital link between past and present, offering a window into the evolving story of the American West. Its programs and events celebrate the enduring spirit and creativity of Western communities, making it a pivotal institution not only for Elko but for the broader understanding of Western American culture.

11.   Cowboy Arts & Gear Museum

Located in Elko, Nevada, the Cowboy Arts & Gear Museum is a tribute to the craftsmanship and heritage of cowboy culture, specifically focusing on the artistry of gear-making that has been passed down through generations. Situated in a beautifully restored building that once housed the historic G.S. Garcia Harness and Saddle Shop, the museum is a cultural treasure that offers a deep dive into the traditional crafts and skills that are integral to cowboy life.

The museum's collections include exquisitely crafted saddles, bridles, spurs, and other pieces of cowboy gear. Each item in the collection tells a story of craftsmanship and practicality, highlighting the functional artistry that cowboys rely on for their daily work. The pieces are not only beautiful but also serve as functional tools that are essential to the cowboy way of life.

Beyond its exhibits, the Cowboy Arts & Gear Museum is a center for education and cultural preservation. It hosts workshops and demonstrations that teach visitors about the techniques and materials used in traditional cowboy gear-making. These workshops are often led by master craftsmen whose expertise adds depth and authenticity to the learning experience.

The museum also explores the impact of the cowboy culture on American history and the continuing influence of this heritage in modern times. Through its programs and collections, the museum fosters an appreciation for the craftsmanship and cultural significance of the cowboy arts, making it an essential visit for anyone interested in the history and culture of the American West.

12.   Northeastern Nevada Museum

The Northeastern Nevada Museum, also located in Elko, provides a comprehensive look at the history, art, and culture of northeastern Nevada. This museum is known for its engaging exhibits that cover a wide range of topics from the natural history of the region to the lives of its people over the centuries.

The museum's historical exhibits include artifacts from the indigenous tribes of the area, early settler life, and the development of industries like mining and ranching that shaped the region's economy and culture. Notably, the museum houses an impressive collection of Basque artifacts, reflecting the significant influence of Basque immigrants on the local culture.

Art enthusiasts will appreciate the museum's art galleries, which feature works by local and regional artists. These galleries showcase a variety of media, reflecting the vibrant artistic community in northeastern Nevada. The museum also hosts traveling exhibits, which bring diverse artistic and cultural perspectives to the community.

For those interested in natural history, the museum offers exhibits on the local flora and fauna, including an impressive array of taxidermy specimens that represent the wildlife of the region. Additionally, the museum features a children's discovery room that offers interactive exhibits designed to make learning fun and engaging for younger visitors.

With its diverse exhibits and educational programs, the Northeastern Nevada Museum plays a crucial role in preserving the region's history and heritage while providing valuable learning resources for the community and visitors alike.

13.   Elko County Fairgrounds

The Elko County Fairgrounds, located in the vibrant city of Elko, Nevada, serves as a central hub for community events, cultural gatherings, and a variety of entertainment options that reflect the rich traditions and dynamic present of the region. As one of the most versatile venues in northeastern Nevada, the fairgrounds host an array of events throughout the year, drawing locals and visitors alike to experience the lively spirit of Elko.

One of the premier events held at the Elko County Fairgrounds is the annual Elko County Fair, a celebration that has been a local tradition for over a century. The fair showcases the agricultural prowess and cowboy heritage of the area, featuring livestock shows, rodeo competitions, and horse races. These events not only highlight the skills and dedication of local farmers and ranchers but also pay homage to the deep-rooted cowboy culture that is integral to the identity of the region.

In addition to the traditional fair activities, the event includes a carnival with a variety of rides and games, arts and crafts exhibits, and food stalls that offer a taste of local cuisine as well as fair favorites. The fairgrounds buzz with live music and performances, creating a festive atmosphere that is perfect for families and visitors of all ages.

The Elko County Fairgrounds are not only active during the fair season but also throughout the year. The facilities are used for a variety of other events, including trade shows, sporting events, and cultural festivals. The grounds feature multiple buildings and outdoor areas that can accommodate everything from large concerts and sports tournaments to more intimate gatherings such as weddings and family reunions.

One of the key features of the fairgrounds is its ability to support large equestrian events. With extensive horse facilities, including stables and a large arena, the fairgrounds are a popular venue for horse shows, roping competitions, and other equestrian activities that draw competitors and spectators from across the state and beyond.

14.   Great Basin College Art Gallery

The Great Basin College Art Gallery, located on the campus of Great Basin College in Elko, Nevada, is a cultural gem that serves both the college community and the public at large. This gallery is dedicated to enriching the cultural landscape of northeastern Nevada by providing a platform for artistic expression and appreciation. Through its exhibitions and programs, the gallery fosters an environment of creativity and dialogue, highlighting works by students, faculty, and regional artists.

The gallery's exhibition schedule is diverse, featuring a range of art forms including paintings, sculpture, photography, and mixed media. These exhibits often explore themes relevant to the Great Basin area, reflecting the landscape, history, and cultural narratives of Nevada and the broader American West. This focus not only serves to inspire local artists but also to engage audiences with the rich artistic traditions and contemporary issues of the region.

In addition to showcasing the work of local and regional artists, the Great Basin College Art Gallery also hosts exhibitions from nationally and internationally recognized artists. These exhibitions provide students and visitors with exposure to a wider range of artistic styles and perspectives, enhancing their understanding and appreciation of global art trends.

Educational programming is a key component of the gallery's mission. The gallery hosts artist talks, workshops, and guided tours that are designed to deepen visitors' understanding of the art on display. These programs are often free and open to the public, providing valuable educational opportunities to the community.

The gallery is also an important educational resource for students of Great Basin College, offering a real-world extension of their classroom learning. Art students are given opportunities to exhibit their work, gaining practical experience in preparing for and setting up exhibitions. This hands-on experience is invaluable as they develop their careers in the arts.

Overall, the Great Basin College Art Gallery plays a pivotal role in promoting the arts in northeastern Nevada. It not only showcases a wide range of artistic talent but also stimulates cultural conversation and education, making it a vital part of the community's cultural fabric.

15. Angel Lake

Angel Lake is a stunning glacial lake nestled at an elevation of 8,378 feet in the East Humboldt Mountain Range near Wells. Known for its striking beauty and serene environment, Angel Lake is a popular destination for those looking to escape the hustle and bustle of daily life and immerse themselves in nature. The lake's crystal-clear waters reflect the surrounding rugged peaks, creating a picturesque setting ideal for photography, painting, or simply soaking in the views.

Recreation opportunities at Angel Lake are plentiful. Fishing is a popular activity, with the lake being regularly stocked with trout, providing anglers with excellent chances of a good catch. The lake's clear, cold waters make it an ideal habitat for trout, and the surrounding scenery adds to the enjoyment of fishing here.

For those who prefer hiking, several trails start at or near Angel Lake, offering varying levels of difficulty and providing stunning views of the lake and the surrounding Humboldt-Toiyabe National Forest. The most popular trail is the Angel Lake Trail, which circles the lake and is easily accessible, making it perfect for families and less experienced hikers. More adventurous hikers might tackle the Greys Lake Trail, a more strenuous hike that leads to a secluded alpine lake at a higher elevation.

Camping is another activity that draws visitors to Angel Lake. The Angel Lake Campground offers developed campsites right by the lake, complete with basic amenities such as picnic tables, fire rings, and restroom facilities. Camping here allows visitors to enjoy the tranquility of the lake during the quieter morning and evening hours.

Angel Lake is not just a summer destination. In the fall, the area is a popular spot for viewing fall foliage, as the quaking aspens and other native trees display vibrant colors. Although the road to Angel Lake closes in winter due to snow, the area is a favorite among backcountry skiers and snowshoers, offering a different kind of beauty and challenge in the snowy season.

16.   Jarbidge Wilderness

The Jarbidge Wilderness, located in remote northern Nevada near the Idaho border, is one of the most isolated and pristine wilderness areas in the United States. Covering over 113,000 acres in the Jarbidge Mountains, it is a sanctuary for adventurous souls seeking solitude and unspoiled natural beauty. Named after the Jarbidge River, which winds through the area, this wilderness provides vital habitat for wildlife and a stunning backdrop for outdoor activities.

The Jarbidge Wilderness boasts a dramatically diverse landscape, from high, snowy peaks and alpine meadows to deep river canyons and dense forests of pine and fir. This variation in elevation supports a rich array of flora and fauna, making it a prime area for wildlife viewing and botanical study. Commonly seen wildlife includes elk, deer, mountain lions, and various bird species.

Hiking and backpacking are popular activities here due to an extensive network of trails that access some of the most remote areas of the American West. Notable trails include the Jarbidge River Trail and the Marys River Trail, which offer challenging hikes through scenic vistas and rugged landscapes. These trails are not well-marked or heavily trafficked, providing a true wilderness experience for those looking to escape the beaten path.

The Jarbidge Wilderness is also a favored destination for experienced hunters and anglers. The area's rivers and streams are renowned for excellent trout fishing, and the vast wilderness provides ideal conditions for big game hunting.

Winter transforms the Jarbidge Wilderness into a snowy wonderland, attracting snowshoeing and cross-country skiing enthusiasts. The deep snow and harsh conditions enhance the solitude and beauty of the wilderness during the winter months.

Camping in the Jarbidge Wilderness is a unique experience, offering a back-to-basics, leave-no-trace adventure. With no developed campsites or facilities, campers must be self-sufficient and respectful of the fragile ecosystem to ensure this wild area remains untouched for future generations.

17.   Wild Horse Reservoir

Wild Horse Reservoir is an enchanting and relatively secluded destination nestled in the high desert region of northern Nevada, approximately 67 miles north of Elko. This scenic area is dominated by the large man-made lake, Wild Horse Reservoir, which was originally constructed in the 1930s and later expanded in 1969. Covering about 2,830 acres when full, the reservoir acts as a popular recreational hub for locals and tourists alike.

The reservoir's clear, cold waters are particularly known for offering excellent fishing opportunities. Anglers are drawn to Wild Horse for its abundant populations of rainbow trout, brown trout, and smallmouth bass. During the winter months, the reservoir becomes a prime spot for ice fishing, providing a unique and serene experience amidst the stark, snowy landscape of the region.

Boating is another popular activity at Wild Horse Reservoir. The expansive water surface accommodates a variety of water sports, from kayaking and canoeing to motorboating. The facility includes well-maintained boat launch areas, making it easy for visitors to access the water and enjoy a day out on the lake.

For those who prefer land-based activities, the surrounding area offers plenty of options. Hiking trails meander through the landscape, offering everything from leisurely walks along the lake's edge to more rigorous hikes up surrounding hillsides, where the rewards include panoramic views of the vast Nevada wilderness. ATV riders also find the open terrain and established trails ideal for exploring the rugged beauty of the area.

Camping near Wild Horse Reservoir is a favorite for many, with developed campsites that provide basic amenities like picnic tables, fire pits, and restrooms. The more adventurous can opt for dispersed camping in more remote sections, enjoying a closer encounter with the wild and pristine environment.

Central Nevada

1. International Car Forest of The Last Church

The International Car Forest of The Last Church stands as one of Nevada's most unique and intriguing art installations, located in the small town of Goldfield. This outdoor exhibition features a bizarre yet fascinating collection of over 40 automobiles, including cars, trucks, and buses, strategically positioned to create an otherworldly landscape. The vehicles are either jutting vertically from the ground or balanced on top of one another, serving as unconventional canvases for artists from around the world.

Created by Mark Rippie and Chad Sorg, the International Car Forest began as a project to break the record for the largest car forest on the planet. However, it quickly evolved into a significant artistic statement about freedom of expression and the ephemeral nature of art. Each vehicle in the forest is painted with elaborate murals, graffiti, and abstract designs, transforming the desert landscape into a sprawling gallery of contemporary art.

Visitors to the Car Forest can wander among the cars, exploring the various themes and artistic styles displayed on each automotive canvas. The experience is surreal, offering a stark contrast between the natural desert environment and the vivid, often thought-provoking artwork. This setting provides not only a backdrop for the art but also contributes to the overall narrative of decay and human impact on nature.

The site has become a magnet for photographers, filmmakers, and creative spirits attracted by its post-apocalyptic ambiance and the freedom it symbolizes. It's a place where art meets the automotive graveyard, inviting reflection on consumer culture, decay, and rebirth through art.

The International Car Forest of The Last Church is free to visit and open year-round, offering an ever-changing exhibit as artists continue to add to and alter the vehicles. It stands as a testament to the transformative power of art and its ability to turn a desolate landscape into a canvas for human expression and creativity.

2.   Tonopah Historic Mining Park

Tonopah Historic Mining Park is a testament to Nevada's rich mining heritage, located on the original site of the Tonopah Mining District. Tonopah, once nicknamed the "Queen of the Silver Camps," played a pivotal role in Nevada's mining boom in the early 20th century. The park covers over 100 acres and preserves many of the original mining structures, equipment, and artifacts that were instrumental in the area's development.

Visitors to the park can explore over three miles of self-guided walking trails that weave through the historic mining landscape. These trails offer access to restored buildings and machinery, including mine shafts, headframes, and ore processing mills. Informative signage along the routes provides historical context, explaining the processes and challenges of silver mining during the boom years.

One of the highlights of the park is the opportunity to visit the underground tunnels where miners toiled to extract silver ore. The Burro Tunnel, for instance, offers guided tours that allow visitors to experience the conditions of underground mining first-hand.

The Tonopah Historic Mining Park also features a Visitor Center, which houses exhibits on the history of the Tonopah Mining District, the lives of miners, and the geological background of the area. These exhibits provide a comprehensive overview of the mining industry's impact on the region and its enduring legacy.

The park is not only an educational resource but also a cultural heritage site that commemorates the hard work and community spirit of the miners who helped shape Nevada's history. Events and workshops are regularly held at the park, including demonstrations of mining techniques and educational programs designed to engage visitors of all ages in the rich history of the area.

3.   Lunar Crater Volcanic Field

The Lunar Crater Volcanic Field is an expansive, otherworldly landscape located in central Nevada, approximately 70 miles east of Tonopah. This remote and rugged area encompasses around 100 square miles and features an impressive array of volcanic features, including cinder cones, lava flows, and the remarkable Lunar Crater, a National Natural Landmark.

Lunar Crater itself is a massive, bowl-shaped depression approximately 430 feet deep and one mile across, formed by explosive volcanic activity. The crater's stark, barren appearance gives the landscape a moon-like quality, which is how it earned its name. Surrounding the crater are various other volcanic cones and vents, each telling a story of the earth's fiery past.

The volcanic field is accessible via a dirt road that leads visitors into the heart of this desolate yet striking landscape. The area offers a unique opportunity for hiking, photography, and geological study. Nature enthusiasts and scientists alike are drawn to the Lunar Crater Volcanic Field for its pristine examples of volcanic formations and the insights they provide into the earth's volcanic processes.

The isolation and minimal light pollution in the area also make it an excellent spot for stargazing. The clear, dark skies offer unparalleled views of the Milky Way and celestial events, adding another layer of attraction to this unique natural area.

4. Mount Jefferson

Mount Jefferson is the highest peak in the Toquima Range and one of the highest in Nevada, standing at an impressive elevation of 11,949 feet. It is located within the Humboldt-Toiyabe National Forest and is split between Nye and Lander counties. The mountain is named after Thomas Jefferson and presents a challenging yet rewarding adventure for hikers and mountaineers.

The mountain is characterized by its rugged terrain, alpine climate, and stunning scenic beauty. There are several routes to the summit, with varying degrees of difficulty, but all offer the opportunity to experience the diverse flora and fauna of the high desert and alpine environments. The summit itself provides breathtaking panoramic views of central Nevada, including distant valleys and surrounding mountain ranges.

Mount Jefferson is also part of the Mount Jefferson Wilderness Area, which encompasses over 18,000 acres. This designation helps protect the area's ecological integrity, including its alpine meadows, aspen groves, and diverse wildlife populations, including mule deer, mountain lions, and various bird species.

The wilderness area is a prime destination for backcountry camping, hiking, and horseback riding, offering a true escape into one of Nevada's most pristine natural environments. The isolation and natural beauty of Mount Jefferson make it a cherished destination for those seeking solitude and a deep connection with nature.

5.   Berlin-Ichthyosaur State Park

Berlin-Ichthyosaur State Park, nestled in the remote central region of Nevada, is a unique combination of historical and paleontological significance. This park protects and interprets the ghost town of Berlin, as well as the largest collection of Ichthyosaur fossils in North America. Established in 1957, the park spans approximately 1,540 acres and offers visitors a glimpse into Nevada's vibrant past—from the age of reptiles to the silver mining boom of the late 19th century.

Berlin, the ghost town within the park, was established in 1897 as part of the Union Mining District. At its peak, Berlin supported a modest community with about 300 residents, influenced largely by the development of the Berlin Mine. Today, visitors can walk through Berlin and see several preserved buildings including miners' cabins, a blacksmith shop, and the assay office, all of which provide a frozen snapshot of life during the mining era. The town's atmosphere is haunting yet fascinating, offering a stark reminder of the boom-and-bust cycles characteristic of Nevada's mining history.

In stark contrast to the human history it preserves, the park is also world-renowned for its paleontological significance due to the Ichthyosaur fossils. Ichthyosaurs were giant marine reptiles that swam in the ocean that covered central Nevada over 225 million years ago during the Triassic period. The park's Fossil House protects and displays these fossils, including a designated National Natural Landmark area where visitors can see several of these ancient creatures preserved in situ. Guided tours of the Fossil House are available, providing insights into the lives of these fascinating marine reptiles and the conditions that preserved their remains so well.

In addition to its historical and paleontological tours, Berlin-Ichthyosaur State Park offers several recreational activities. The park's high desert landscape is ideal for hiking, with trails that wander through the hills offering panoramic views of the surrounding basin and range topography. The park's elevation makes it a cool retreat during the summer, and its clear, dark skies are perfect for stargazing, away from the light pollution of larger cities.

6.   Toquima Cave Art

Toquima Cave, located within the scenic Toquima Range and nestled in central Nevada's vast landscape, is a significant archaeological site known for its remarkable ancient rock art. This secluded cave is not only a spiritual site but also a canvas that offers insight into the lives and beliefs of the Native American peoples who inhabited the region thousands of years ago.

The cave's interior walls are adorned with pictographs that are considered some of the finest examples of ancient American Indian rock art in Nevada. These paintings, which are believed to have been created by the ancestors of the contemporary Shoshone people, feature a variety of designs including abstract patterns and figures. The colors used in these pictographs—red, white, black, and yellow—are derived from natural pigments found in the surrounding area, and they have endured the test of time remarkably well.

Archaeologists believe that Toquima Cave's art was primarily spiritual or ceremonial in nature, possibly relating to the practices of vision quests or other rites of passage. This interpretation is supported by the secluded and high location of the cave, which would have made it an ideal site for such spiritual activities.

Visiting Toquima Cave provides a profound connection to the past, allowing one to stand in the same spots where ancient peoples once gathered, lived, and expressed themselves artistically. The site is accessible via a dirt road followed by a short hike, which adds to the sense of adventure and isolation one feels when visiting. The surrounding area is also rich in wildlife and native plants, adding to the overall experience of visiting this historic site.

Preservation efforts are crucial in maintaining the integrity of Toquima Cave and its artwork. Visitors are encouraged to view the art respectfully and leave no trace, ensuring that this cultural treasure remains intact for future generations to learn from and enjoy.

7.   Stokes Castle

Stokes Castle, located in Austin, Nevada, is a fascinating historical landmark that stands as a testament to the mining boom that swept through Nevada in the late 19th century. Built in 1897 by Anson Phelps Stokes, a wealthy mine developer, banker, and railroad magnate, the castle is a three-story stone tower that overlooks the Reese River Valley.

Constructed using native granite hewn from the nearby hills, the design of Stokes Castle was inspired by a Roman tower that Stokes admired during his travels in Italy. The castle was intended as a summer home for the Stokes family to entertain guests and enjoy the Nevada landscape. However, the family used it for only a short time before leaving the area.

Today, Stokes Castle stands as an iconic ruin. Its stone walls and empty window frames create a picturesque silhouette against the vast Nevada sky, especially striking at sunset. The structure offers a glimpse into the personal lives of those who were part of Nevada's mining elite, contrasting sharply with the typically modest living conditions of miners and other local workers of the era.

Preservation efforts have maintained the stability of the structure, allowing visitors to explore the exterior of the castle and enjoy panoramic views of the valley below. Informational signage at the site provides historical context and shares details about the castle's construction, its brief period of use, and its significance to the local community.

Visiting Stokes Castle is a journey into Nevada's rich mining history, offering insights into the aspirations and lifestyles of its historical figures. The castle's unique architecture and its enduring presence in the Nevada landscape make it a compelling destination for history enthusiasts and those interested in the legacy of the American West.

8.   Eureka Opera House

The Eureka Opera House is a historic gem located in Eureka, Nevada, a town that flourished during the silver mining boom in the 19th century. Originally built in 1880, the opera house served as a cultural center for the thriving mining community, hosting a variety of performances, town meetings, and social gatherings.

After falling into disrepair, the Eureka Opera House was beautifully restored in the 1990s to its former glory, retaining much of its original charm and Victorian elegance. The restoration included the refurbishment of the ornate interior, complete with period-appropriate decor, red velvet curtains, and wooden stage, transporting visitors back in time.

Today, the Eureka Opera House is once again a vibrant center for the arts and community events in Eureka. It hosts concerts, theatrical performances, conferences, and weddings, serving as a focal point for cultural activity in the area. The opera house is also open for tours, allowing visitors to explore its historic auditorium, balcony, and stage, where local lore whispers of past performances by traveling vaudeville troupes and famous operatic talents.

The Eureka Opera House not only offers a window into the cultural life of a bygone era but also plays a crucial role in the preservation and celebration of local history and the arts. It stands as a testament to the community's commitment to restoring and maintaining its historical landmarks, making it a must-visit for those traveling through Nevada's scenic heartland.

9.   Illipah Reservoir

Illipah Reservoir, situated in White Pine County, Nevada, is a hidden gem that offers a serene and picturesque setting for outdoor enthusiasts. Located approximately 40 miles west of Ely along Highway 50, also known as the Loneliest Road in America, this reservoir is a popular destination for fishing, camping, and wildlife observation. Created in 1953 for irrigation purposes, Illipah Reservoir has since become a haven for recreational activities, attracting visitors seeking tranquility amidst Nevada's high desert landscape.

The reservoir spans about 70 acres and is known for its excellent fishing opportunities. Anglers frequent Illipah for its healthy populations of rainbow and brown trout, which are stocked regularly by the Nevada Department of Wildlife. The reservoir's clear, cold waters provide an ideal habitat for these fish, making it a prime spot for both shore and boat fishing. Fly fishing is particularly popular here, with the serene waters offering a perfect backdrop for a day of angling.

Camping is another major draw to Illipah Reservoir. The surrounding area offers primitive camping sites that are free of charge and available on a first-come, first-served basis. These sites are equipped with basic amenities such as picnic tables and fire rings, making them perfect for a rustic camping experience. The wide-open spaces and lack of light pollution make it an excellent spot for stargazing, providing campers with breathtaking night skies.

Hiking and wildlife observation are also popular activities around Illipah Reservoir. The area is home to a variety of wildlife, including mule deer, antelope, and numerous bird species. The open desert and mountainous backdrop create a stunning landscape that is ideal for photography and nature walks. Visitors can explore the surrounding hills and valleys, enjoying the peace and solitude of the Nevada wilderness.

The reservoir is accessible year-round, but the best times to visit are during the spring and fall when the weather is mild and the scenery is particularly beautiful. In the winter, the area can be quite cold and the reservoir may freeze over, creating a different but equally enchanting landscape.

10. Ward Mountain Recreation Area

The Ward Mountain Recreation Area, located a few miles west of Ely, Nevada, offers diverse outdoor activities against the stunning backdrop of the Egan Range. Part of the Humboldt-Toiyabe National Forest, this recreation area provides hiking, camping, mountain biking, and winter sports opportunities, making it a year-round destination for adventure seekers and nature lovers.

One of the key attractions is its extensive network of trails, catering to hikers, mountain bikers, and equestrians. The trails range from easy walks to challenging climbs, winding through dense pinyon-juniper forests and open meadows, offering breathtaking views of the surrounding mountains and valleys. The Ward Mountain Loop Trail is particularly popular for its scenic vistas and diverse terrain.

Camping at Ward Mountain is a favorite activity, with well-maintained campgrounds offering amenities like picnic tables, fire rings, and restrooms. Set in tranquil forested areas, the campgrounds provide a peaceful retreat with clear night skies perfect for stargazing and cool mountain air offering a refreshing escape from the summer heat.

Mountain biking enthusiasts will find the trails accommodating various skill levels, from beginners to advanced riders. The rugged terrain and elevation changes provide a thrilling ride, complemented by the scenic beauty of the area and opportunities to spot wildlife.

In winter, Ward Mountain transforms into a snowy wonderland, attracting cross-country skiers and snowshoers. The serene, snow-covered landscape is perfect for winter sports, offering a quiet and picturesque environment.

Wildlife observation is popular at Ward Mountain, home to mule deer, mountain lions, and numerous bird species. Birdwatchers can spot hawks, eagles, and other birds of prey, while hikers may encounter deer and other animals along the trails.

The nearby Ward Charcoal Ovens State Historic Park features six well-preserved beehive-shaped charcoal ovens from the late 19th century, providing a glimpse into Nevada's mining history and enhancing the area's historical significance.

11.   White Pine Public Museum

The White Pine Public Museum, located in Ely, Nevada, is a treasure trove of local history and culture, offering visitors a fascinating glimpse into the past of White Pine County and the surrounding region. Established in 1959, the museum preserves and showcases the area's rich heritage through a diverse collection of artifacts, exhibits, and historical buildings.

One of the museum's most significant attractions is its extensive collection of mining artifacts. The museum features tools, equipment, and memorabilia from the area's mining boom, illustrating the various mining techniques used over the years and the challenges faced by miners.

In addition to mining artifacts, the White Pine Public Museum houses an impressive collection of prehistoric fossils and Native American artifacts. The paleontological exhibits include fossils of ancient marine life, while the Native American artifacts, such as pottery and arrowheads, highlight the rich cultural heritage of the region's original inhabitants.

The museum also features exhibits on the early settlers of White Pine County, showcasing the daily lives of pioneers. Visitors can explore a replica pioneer cabin, complete with period furnishings, and view a collection of photographs and documents that provide historical context for the artifacts on display.

A unique aspect of the museum is its outdoor exhibit area, which includes several historic buildings relocated to the museum grounds, such as the McGill Depot and the Cherry Creek Schoolhouse. These buildings offer an immersive experience, allowing visitors to step back in time and explore significant historical structures.

The museum also features a charming gift shop offering books, souvenirs, and locally made crafts, allowing visitors to take home a piece of White Pine County's history while supporting the museum's preservation efforts.

12. Nevada Northern Railway Museum

The Nevada Northern Railway Museum, located in Ely, Nevada, is a living testament to the golden age of railroading in the American West. Established in 1983, the museum preserves the historic Nevada Northern Railway, which played a crucial role in the region's early 20th-century development. Visitors can step back in time and experience vintage rail travel's excitement and romance.

The museum's centerpiece is its impressive collection of historic locomotives and railcars. It boasts one of the best-preserved historic railroads in the United States, complete with its original depot, engine house, and rolling stock. Visitors can explore meticulously restored steam and diesel locomotives, passenger cars, and freight cars, offering a fascinating look at the technology and craftsmanship that powered the railroads.

A highlight of the Nevada Northern Railway Museum is the opportunity to ride historic trains. The museum offers regularly scheduled excursion trains along the original routes, providing scenic journeys through eastern Nevada's stunning landscapes. These rides use vintage locomotives and railcars, offering an authentic railroading experience complete with the sights, sounds, and smells of a bygone era.

The museum also offers themed train rides throughout the year, such as the Polar Express during the holiday season, wildflower tours, photography excursions, and star-gazing trains. These unique experiences showcase the beauty and history of the region.

In addition to rail operations, the museum features exhibits and displays that tell the story of the railroad and its impact on the local community. The interpretive center includes photographs, documents, and artifacts detailing the Nevada Northern Railway's history and its role in transporting copper ore from White Pine County's mines.

Visitors can explore the museum's maintenance and restoration facilities, where skilled craftsmen and volunteers work to preserve historic locomotives and railcars. Guided tours of the engine house and machine shop offer a behind-the-scenes look at the intricate processes involved in maintaining vintage equipment.

13.   Ely Railroad Depot Museum

The Ely Railroad Depot Museum, located in Ely, Nevada, is dedicated to preserving and showcasing the rich history of railroading in the region. Housed in the historic Nevada Northern Railway Depot, built in 1907, the museum highlights the pivotal role the railroad played in the development of Ely and surrounding areas.

Visitors are greeted by exhibits that delve into the history of the Nevada Northern Railway, which transported copper ore from White Pine County's mines to markets nationwide. Displays include vintage photographs, railroad tools, and equipment, providing a comprehensive look at the daily operations and challenges of running a railroad during its peak years.

A standout feature of the museum is its collection of restored locomotives and railcars, some of which are still operational. These pieces offer a tangible connection to the past, allowing visitors to appreciate the engineering marvels of their time. Guided tours provide insights into the construction, functionality, and economic impact of these historic trains.

The museum also emphasizes the human aspect of railroad history. Exhibits dedicated to the workers who built and maintained the railway offer glimpses into their lives through personal stories, letters, and artifacts. This helps paint a vivid picture of the community that grew around the railroad industry.

Interactive experiences are a highlight, including hands-on activities like telegraphy demonstrations that teach visitors about early 20th-century railroad communication methods. Educational programs and workshops for all ages make the museum a valuable resource for learning about industrial history and railroading.

Conveniently located in the heart of Ely and close to the Nevada Northern Railway Museum, the Ely Railroad Depot Museum provides a comprehensive tour of Ely's railroading history. Visitors can ride historic trains and explore extensive rail yards and facilities.

14.   McGill Drugstore Museum

The McGill Drugstore Museum, located in the small town of McGill, Nevada, is a remarkable time capsule offering visitors a glimpse into the past. Once a bustling community hub, the drugstore operated from the early 20th century until its closure in the 1970s. Today, it stands as a meticulously preserved museum, providing a unique window into the daily lives and healthcare practices of a bygone era.

Stepping into the McGill Drugstore Museum is like stepping back in time. The interior of the store has been preserved exactly as it was when it closed, with shelves stocked with original products, medicines, and everyday items from the mid-20th century. This incredible attention to detail creates an authentic and immersive experience for visitors, allowing them to see and feel what it was like to shop in a small-town drugstore decades ago.

The museum's collection includes a wide array of pharmaceutical items, from patent medicines and tonics to prescription drugs and medical equipment. These items offer fascinating insights into the medical practices and health beliefs of the early to mid-20th century. Visitors can see everything from old-fashioned remedies and herbal medicines to the early forms of now-common pharmaceuticals.

In addition to its pharmaceutical displays, the McGill Drugstore Museum features a range of everyday products that were sold in the store. These include toiletries, cosmetics, candy, and tobacco products, reflecting the consumer culture of the time. The store's soda fountain, a common feature in drugstores of the era, is also preserved and is a highlight of the museum. It serves as a nostalgic reminder of when the drugstore was a social gathering place as well as a retail establishment.

The museum also sheds light on the role of the pharmacist in the community. As one of the most trusted figures in small towns, the pharmacist was often the first point of contact for medical advice and minor health concerns. The museum's exhibits include personal artifacts and documents from the pharmacists who worked in the store, providing a deeper understanding of their daily responsibilities and the important role they played in the community.

15. Cave Lake State Park

Cave Lake State Park, located in the Schell Creek Range of eastern Nevada, is a stunning natural retreat offering diverse outdoor activities and breathtaking scenery. Situated about 15 miles southeast of Ely, this 4,500-acre park centers around the picturesque Cave Lake, a 32-acre reservoir that provides year-round recreation.

Fishing is a main attraction at Cave Lake, regularly stocked with rainbow and brown trout. Whether from shore or boat, anglers enjoy the serene environment, and ice fishing is popular during the winter months when the lake freezes over.

Camping is another draw, with two developed campgrounds—Elk Flat and Lake View—offering amenities like picnic tables, fire rings, and restrooms. These campgrounds provide beautiful views of the lake and mountains. For a more primitive experience, dispersed camping areas offer seclusion and a natural setting.

Hiking and mountain biking are popular, with trails winding through rugged terrain and offering spectacular vistas. The Cave Lake Overlook Trail provides a moderate hike with panoramic views, while the Steptoe Creek Trail takes hikers through lush forests and along a scenic creek.

In winter, the park transforms into a wonderland, attracting snowshoeing, cross-country skiing, and ice skating enthusiasts. The annual Fire and Ice Winter Festival features ice sculpting, fireworks, and winter sports competitions, adding a festive atmosphere to the tranquil landscape.

Wildlife viewing is abundant, with diverse habitats supporting mule deer, elk, mountain lions, and numerous bird species. Birdwatchers can spot raptors, songbirds, and waterfowl around the lake and surrounding areas.

The park's visitor center provides information about the natural and cultural history of the area, as well as details on recreational opportunities. Rangers offer guidance to ensure a safe and enjoyable visit.

16.   Cave Valley

Cave Valley, located in eastern Nevada's scenic Great Basin, is a hidden gem offering natural beauty, outdoor adventure, and historical intrigue. Nestled within the Humboldt-Toiyabe National Forest, the valley is characterized by rugged terrain, dramatic cliffs, and vast expanses of sagebrush and juniper.

A primary attraction of Cave Valley is its numerous caves, formed by ancient geological processes. These range from small rock shelters to extensive underground networks like Whipple Cave, known for its impressive limestone formations. While some caves are accessible for casual exploration, others require technical skills, attracting experienced cavers and spelunkers.

Hiking and horseback riding are popular activities, with several trails traversing the diverse landscapes. These trails offer opportunities to see wildlife such as mule deer, pronghorn antelope, and various bird species. The solitude and serenity of the valley make it ideal for escaping crowds and enjoying peaceful outdoor experiences.

Cave Valley is rich in historical and cultural significance, with evidence of Native American habitation for thousands of years. Rock art and artifacts, including petroglyphs and pictographs, adorn some rock faces and caves, providing a glimpse into the lives and beliefs of the early inhabitants.

Camping in Cave Valley offers a primitive and secluded experience, with several dispersed sites allowing visitors to immerse themselves in nature. The lack of light pollution makes it an excellent spot for stargazing, with clear night skies offering breathtaking views of the Milky Way.

Due to its remote location, visitors must be well-prepared and self-sufficient, bringing all necessary supplies, including water, food, and camping gear. Despite the lack of amenities, the rewards of exploring Cave Valley are well worth the effort.

Cave Valley is also a great destination for geology and natural history enthusiasts. The unique rock formations and caves offer excellent opportunities to study geological processes.

17.   Ward Charcoal Ovens State Historic Park

Ward Charcoal Ovens State Historic Park, located in the Egan Mountain Range near Ely, Nevada, is a fascinating destination that combines natural beauty with historical intrigue. This 700-acre park is home to six well-preserved beehive-shaped charcoal ovens, which were constructed in the late 19th century to produce charcoal for the nearby silver mining operations in Ward, a bustling mining town during that era.

The charcoal ovens, built in 1876, are the park's main attraction. Standing about 30 feet high and 27 feet in diameter, these stone structures are an impressive testament to the ingenuity of early industrial processes. They were used to convert locally harvested wood into charcoal, a necessary fuel for the smelting of silver ore. The high-quality charcoal produced here was essential for the efficient extraction of silver from the mined ore, making these ovens a vital part of the mining operations in Ward.

Visitors to the park can explore these historic structures up close and learn about their significance through informative plaques and displays. The ovens' unique design and construction are fascinating to observe, and they offer a glimpse into the arduous labor and resourcefulness of the miners and workers who built and operated them. The ovens have been well-preserved, and their remarkable state of preservation offers a rare opportunity to experience a piece of Nevada's industrial history firsthand.

In addition to the historic charcoal ovens, the park offers a variety of recreational activities. There are several hiking trails that wind through the surrounding pinyon-juniper woodlands and sagebrush-covered hills, providing stunning views of the Egan Range and the expansive high desert landscape. These trails are perfect for nature walks, birdwatching, and photography, offering a peaceful and scenic retreat from the hustle and bustle of everyday life.

Ward Charcoal Ovens State Historic Park also features picnic areas with tables and grills, making it an ideal spot for a family outing or a relaxing day in nature. The park's remote location and dark skies make it an excellent destination for stargazing, providing breathtaking views of the Milky Way and other celestial wonders.

18.   Mount Moriah Wilderness

The Mount Moriah Wilderness, located in the Snake Range of eastern Nevada, is a pristine and rugged wilderness area that offers a true escape into nature's untouched beauty. Covering approximately 89,000 acres, this wilderness area is managed by the U.S. Forest Service and is part of the Humboldt-Toiyabe National Forest. It is renowned for its dramatic landscapes, diverse ecosystems, and opportunities for solitude and adventure.

Mount Moriah, the centerpiece of the wilderness, stands at an impressive elevation of 12,067 feet, making it one of the highest peaks in Nevada. The mountain and its surrounding area are characterized by steep canyons, alpine meadows, and dense forests of pinyon pine, juniper, and bristlecone pine. The varied terrain supports a rich diversity of flora and fauna, making it a haven for wildlife enthusiasts and naturalists.

Hiking and backpacking are among the most popular activities in the Mount Moriah Wilderness. Numerous trails traverse the wilderness, ranging from challenging climbs to the summit of Mount Moriah to more moderate hikes through the scenic valleys and forests. The Hendry's Creek Trail and the Hampton Creek Trail are two notable routes that offer stunning views and access to remote parts of the wilderness. These trails provide hikers with the opportunity to experience the serene beauty of the area and encounter its diverse wildlife, including mule deer, mountain lions, and various bird species.

The wilderness is also home to several groves of ancient bristlecone pines, some of the oldest living trees on earth. These trees, with their gnarled and twisted forms, add a unique and mystical quality to the landscape. Visitors to the bristlecone groves can marvel at the resilience and longevity of these remarkable trees, some of which are thousands of years old.

For those seeking a more immersive experience, the Mount Moriah Wilderness offers excellent opportunities for backcountry camping. The remote and undeveloped nature of the area means that campers can enjoy a true wilderness experience, far from the noise and distractions of modern life. The clear night skies, free from light pollution, provide spectacular stargazing opportunities, making camping in this wilderness a truly magical experience.

68

19. Baker Archaeological Site

The Baker Archaeological Site, near Baker in eastern Nevada, offers insights into the ancient history and cultures of the Great Basin region. Also known as Baker Village, this significant archaeological area was inhabited by the Fremont people between approximately 1220 and 1295 AD.

Discovered in the 1950s and extensively excavated in the 1990s, the site reveals a wealth of information about the Fremont people's way of life. Visitors can explore remains of structures, including pit houses, surface dwellings, and storage facilities, along with numerous artifacts. These elements provide a glimpse into the daily lives of the ancient inhabitants.

The interpretive trails at the Baker Archaeological Site offer a self-guided tour of key features. Informative signs and displays provide context about the construction and use of the structures, tools, artifacts, and agricultural practices of the Fremont people. A highlight is the reconstructed pit house, a replica of a typical Fremont dwelling, offering a tangible connection to the past.

Situated near the entrance to Great Basin National Park, the site combines archaeological significance with natural beauty, offering stunning views of the surrounding mountains and valleys. This blend makes it a compelling destination for those interested in both history and the outdoors.

The site hosts educational programs and events, including guided tours, lectures, and hands-on activities, aimed at engaging the public with the history and archaeology of the Great Basin. These programs provide a deeper understanding of the Fremont culture and the importance of archaeological preservation.

Managed by the National Park Service in conjunction with Great Basin National Park, the site is preserved and maintained for future generations. Efforts to protect and interpret the site reflect a commitment to preserving the rich cultural heritage of the Great Basin region.

20. Great Basin National Park

Great Basin National Park, located in eastern Nevada near the Utah border, is a spectacular natural wonder showcasing the diverse landscapes and rich biodiversity of the Great Basin region. Established in 1986, the park covers over 77,000 acres and offers a wide array of outdoor activities, stunning scenery, and unique geological features. It is one of the least crowded national parks in the U.S., providing a serene environment for exploration and adventure.

One of the park's most prominent features is Wheeler Peak, which stands at 13,063 feet, offering breathtaking views of surrounding valleys and mountain ranges. The Wheeler Peak Scenic Drive provides access to trailheads and viewpoints, making it a popular route for experiencing the park's high-altitude beauty.

Hiking is a main attraction, with numerous trails catering to all skill levels. The Bristlecone Pine Trail leads hikers through ancient groves of bristlecone pines, some over 5,000 years old. The Alpine Lakes Loop takes hikers to the picturesque Stella and Teresa Lakes, offering stunning views of the alpine landscape. For a more challenging adventure, the Wheeler Peak Summit Trail provides a strenuous but rewarding climb to the summit.

The park is also home to Lehman Caves, a series of limestone caverns adorned with intricate formations such as stalactites, stalagmites, and helictites. Guided tours offer an in-depth look at the geology and history of these stunning caves.

Wildlife enthusiasts can observe a variety of species, including mule deer, mountain lions, marmots, and numerous bird species. Birdwatchers can spot raptors, songbirds, and waterfowl around the park's streams and wetlands.

Renowned for its dark skies, Great Basin National Park is an exceptional destination for stargazing, with minimal light pollution providing excellent opportunities to observe stars, planets, and celestial phenomena. The park hosts astronomy programs and events to enhance the stargazing experience.

Camping is popular, with several campgrounds offering a range of amenities. The cool mountain air and scenic surroundings make camping a memorable experience.

21.   Spring Valley State Park

Spring Valley State Park, located in eastern Nevada near the town of Pioche, offers a picturesque retreat with diverse recreational opportunities. This 1,281-acre park is centered around the 65-acre Eagle Valley Reservoir, providing a scenic backdrop for various outdoor activities. The park's lush meadows, rolling hills, and rocky outcrops create a stunning contrast against Nevada's typically arid landscape.

Fishing is a major draw at Spring Valley State Park, with the reservoir being stocked regularly with rainbow trout, tiger trout, and other species. Anglers can enjoy the serene environment while trying their luck from the shore or a boat. The park also offers a boat launch and docks for easy water access.

Camping facilities are well-developed, featuring two campgrounds with a total of 37 sites, including RV sites with hookups. The campsites are equipped with picnic tables, fire rings, and restrooms, providing a comfortable setting for overnight stays. The lush surroundings and abundant wildlife make camping here a delightful experience.

Hiking and wildlife viewing are popular activities within the park. Several trails meander through the varied terrain, offering opportunities to explore the area's natural beauty and spot local wildlife such as mule deer, rabbits, and numerous bird species. The park's diverse habitats support a wide range of flora and fauna, making it a great destination for nature enthusiasts.

Spring Valley State Park also boasts a rich history, with remnants of 19th-century settlements and ranches scattered throughout the area. Visitors can explore historical sites like the Stone Cabin, built by early settlers, and the historic cemeteries that provide a glimpse into the lives of the pioneers who once inhabited the region.

The park is open year-round, offering seasonal activities such as ice fishing and snowshoeing in the winter, making it a versatile destination for outdoor recreation. Whether you're looking to fish, hike, camp, or simply enjoy the tranquil scenery, Spring Valley State Park provides a serene escape in the heart of Nevada's wilderness.

22.   Pioche Ghost Town

Pioche, once a booming mining town in eastern Nevada, is now a fascinating ghost town that offers visitors a glimpse into the tumultuous history of the American West. Founded in the 1860s after the discovery of silver ore, Pioche quickly grew into one of the most notorious and lawless towns of the mining frontier. At its peak, it was one of Nevada's largest and wealthiest communities.

Today, Pioche retains much of its Wild West charm, with numerous historic buildings and relics from its mining heyday. The town's main street is lined with old saloons, storefronts, and other structures that evoke the spirit of the 19th century. The preserved architecture and remnants of the past create an atmospheric setting for exploration.

One of Pioche's most notable landmarks is the Million Dollar Courthouse, completed in 1872. Despite its name, the courthouse's actual construction cost was around $88,000, but due to financing complications, the final cost ballooned to nearly a million dollars over the years. Today, it serves as a museum, offering exhibits on local history and the town's notorious past.

Another highlight is Boot Hill Cemetery, where many of the town's early residents, including outlaws and gunfighters, are buried. The cemetery provides a poignant reminder of the town's violent and often tragic history, with many graves marked by simple wooden crosses and weathered headstones.

Pioche is also home to the historic Overland Hotel, which has been restored and now operates as a bed and breakfast, allowing visitors to experience a taste of the past while enjoying modern comforts. The hotel, along with other historic buildings, adds to the town's unique character and appeal.

Visitors to Pioche can explore the remnants of old mining operations, including headframes, ore bins, and other equipment scattered throughout the hillsides. The nearby Pioche Mining District offers additional opportunities for hiking and exploring the rugged landscape.

Overall, Pioche Ghost Town provides a captivating journey into the past, with its rich history, preserved architecture, and scenic surroundings.

23.   Echo Canyon State Park

Echo Canyon State Park, located near the town of Pioche in southeastern Nevada, is a serene and scenic destination known for its rugged beauty and diverse recreational opportunities. The park encompasses 1,800 acres and is centered around the picturesque Echo Canyon Reservoir, a popular spot for fishing, boating, and wildlife viewing.

The reservoir is stocked with rainbow trout, crappie, and largemouth bass, making it a favorite among anglers. Fishing from the shore or by boat offers a peaceful way to enjoy the stunning surroundings. The park provides a boat launch, making it easy for visitors to get out on the water.

Camping is a highlight at Echo Canyon State Park, with a well-maintained campground offering 33 campsites equipped with picnic tables, fire pits, and shade structures. The campground includes amenities such as restrooms and showers, ensuring a comfortable stay for visitors. The scenic setting, with views of the reservoir and surrounding hills, makes camping here a delightful experience.

Hiking trails in the park offer opportunities to explore the diverse landscape, which includes dramatic rock formations, lush meadows, and sagebrush-covered hills. The Ash Canyon Trail is a popular route that takes hikers through a narrow canyon with striking geological features and offers stunning views of the Echo Canyon Reservoir.

Wildlife viewing is another attraction, with the park being home to a variety of species, including mule deer, coyotes, and numerous bird species. Birdwatchers can spot hawks, eagles, and waterfowl, particularly around the reservoir and wetlands.

The park's visitor center provides information about the area's natural and cultural history, including the history of the Paiute people who once inhabited the region. The center offers educational displays and resources for visitors interested in learning more about the park and its surroundings.

24.   Cathedral Gorge State Park

Cathedral Gorge State Park, located in southeastern Nevada near the town of Panaca, is renowned for its dramatic and unique landscape, characterized by towering spires and intricate formations carved into soft bentonite clay. This 1,608-acre park offers visitors a chance to explore one of Nevada's most stunning and geologically intriguing environments.

The park's landscape was formed millions of years ago during the Pliocene Epoch, when volcanic activity and subsequent erosion created the distinctive narrow canyons and cathedral-like spires. The result is a maze of slot canyons and sculpted clay formations that invite exploration and discovery. The surreal, almost otherworldly terrain makes Cathedral Gorge a paradise for photographers and nature enthusiasts.

Hiking is a primary activity at Cathedral Gorge State Park, with several trails that meander through the fascinating landscape. The Miller Point Trail is a popular choice, offering panoramic views of the gorge from an overlook before descending into the labyrinth of narrow canyons below. Another notable trail is the Juniper Draw Loop, which provides a more comprehensive tour of the park's varied topography and geological features.

The park also features a well-equipped campground with 22 campsites that include amenities such as picnic tables, fire rings, and shade structures. The campground is open year-round and offers a serene setting for visitors to enjoy the park's natural beauty. Modern restrooms and showers add to the comfort and convenience of camping at Cathedral Gorge.

For those interested in learning more about the park's unique geology and history, the visitor center provides informative exhibits and displays. Interpretive programs and guided tours are also available, offering deeper insights into the formation of the landscape and the natural processes at work.

Picnicking is another popular activity, with shaded picnic areas that offer stunning views of the surrounding formations. These areas are perfect for a family outing or a relaxing meal amidst the park's striking scenery.

25. Kershaw-Ryan State Park

Kershaw-Ryan State Park, located near Caliente in southeastern Nevada, is a verdant oasis set against the rugged backdrop of the Mojave Desert. Covering 265 acres, the park is known for its lush gardens, scenic canyon, and vibrant wildlife, offering a refreshing escape into nature.

The park's centerpiece is its beautifully maintained picnic area, surrounded by terraced gardens filled with native and introduced plant species. Visitors can relax in the shaded picnic spots, enjoy the soothing sounds of natural springs, and explore the gardens that bloom with colorful flowers and lush greenery, a stark contrast to the surrounding desert landscape.

Hiking is a popular activity at Kershaw-Ryan State Park. The Rattlesnake Canyon Trail, a moderate hike, takes visitors through a narrow canyon with stunning rock formations and panoramic views of the surrounding area. The trail provides an excellent opportunity to observe the diverse plant life and wildlife that inhabit the park, including birds, lizards, and the occasional deer.

The park also features a natural spring-fed wading pool, perfect for cooling off during the hot summer months. This family-friendly spot is a favorite among visitors, offering a refreshing way to enjoy the park's natural beauty. The nearby playground provides additional entertainment for children, making the park an ideal destination for family outings.

Camping is available at Kershaw-Ryan State Park, with campsites equipped with picnic tables, fire rings, and nearby restrooms. The campground offers a peaceful setting for an overnight stay, with the chance to enjoy stargazing under the clear desert skies, free from light pollution.

Kershaw-Ryan State Park also holds historical significance. The park's namesakes, Samuel and Hannah Kershaw, established a ranch here in the late 1800s. The park's history is commemorated through interpretive displays that provide insights into the lives of early settlers in the area.

In summary, Kershaw-Ryan State Park is a delightful destination that combines natural beauty, recreational activities, and historical significance.

26.   Beaver Dam State Park

Beaver Dam State Park, located in eastern Nevada near the Utah border, is a hidden gem known for its scenic beauty, rugged terrain, and abundant wildlife. Spanning over 2,000 acres, the park offers a tranquil retreat where visitors can engage in a variety of outdoor activities amidst stunning natural surroundings.

The park is named after the historic beaver dams that once dotted the area. Today, it features a picturesque landscape of canyons, streams, and woodlands. Pine Park Canyon, the park's primary feature, is carved by Beaver Dam Wash and offers dramatic views of eroded rock formations and lush vegetation.

Fishing is a major draw at Beaver Dam State Park. Schroeder Reservoir, fed by Beaver Dam Wash, is stocked with rainbow trout, providing excellent fishing opportunities. Anglers can enjoy the serene environment while trying their luck from the shore or a small boat. The park's streams also offer fly fishing prospects, adding to the appeal for fishing enthusiasts.

Hiking trails traverse the park's diverse terrain, offering routes for both casual walkers and avid hikers. The Oak Knoll Trail is a popular choice, leading visitors through pinyon-juniper woodlands and offering breathtaking views of the surrounding landscape. The varied trails provide opportunities to explore the park's natural beauty and spot wildlife such as mule deer, wild turkeys, and numerous bird species.

Camping at Beaver Dam State Park is a peaceful experience, with two campgrounds providing sites equipped with picnic tables, fire pits, and nearby restrooms. The remote location ensures a quiet and undisturbed stay, perfect for those looking to escape the hustle and bustle of everyday life. The park's elevation and clear skies make it an ideal spot for stargazing.

In addition to its natural attractions, Beaver Dam State Park is rich in history. The area was once inhabited by Native American tribes, and evidence of their presence can still be found. The park also played a role in the early ranching and mining history of the region, adding a historical dimension to its appeal.

27. Pahranagat National Wildlife Refuge

Pahranagat National Wildlife Refuge, located in southern Nevada near Alamo, is a haven for wildlife and a sanctuary for nature lovers. Established in 1963, the refuge spans over 5,380 acres and includes a diverse array of habitats such as wetlands, lakes, meadows, and desert landscapes. This unique blend of environments makes it an ideal spot for birdwatching, photography, and outdoor recreation.

The refuge is a critical stopover for migratory birds along the Pacific Flyway. Each year, thousands of birds, including waterfowl, raptors, and songbirds, visit Pahranagat, making it a paradise for birdwatchers. Notable species include the American white pelican, bald eagle, and various ducks and geese. The refuge's wetlands provide essential breeding and feeding grounds, supporting a rich diversity of avian life.

Fishing is another popular activity at Pahranagat National Wildlife Refuge. The refuge's lakes and ponds are home to largemouth bass, crappie, and catfish. Anglers can enjoy fishing from the shore or from small boats, surrounded by the tranquil beauty of the refuge.

Hiking trails throughout the refuge offer opportunities to explore its diverse landscapes. The Upper Lake Trail and Marsh Trail are particularly popular, providing access to the wetlands and offering excellent wildlife viewing opportunities. The trails are relatively easy, making them suitable for visitors of all ages and fitness levels.

Camping is available at the refuge, with designated primitive campsites that provide a rustic and serene experience. The campsites are free of charge and are available on a first-come, first-served basis. The remote location and lack of light pollution make the refuge an excellent spot for stargazing, offering clear views of the night sky.

Pahranagat National Wildlife Refuge also serves an important educational role, with a visitor center that offers exhibits and information about the refuge's ecosystems and the species that inhabit them. Educational programs and guided tours are available, providing deeper insights into the importance of conservation and the refuge's role in protecting wildlife.

Las Vegas and Southern Nevada

1.   Valley of Fire State Park

Valley of Fire State Park, located in the Mojave Desert of Nevada, is the state's oldest and largest state park, renowned for its vibrant red sandstone formations that appear to be on fire during sunset, hence its name. Established in 1935, the park spans over 40,000 acres and is a haven for geology enthusiasts, photographers, and outdoor adventurers. The landscape, sculpted over 150 million years through erosion and shifting sand dunes, offers a glimpse into the ancient world with its petrified trees and petroglyphs left by Native American tribes, primarily the Ancestral Puebloans.

Hiking is a popular activity in the Valley of Fire, with trails like the Fire Wave Trail, which leads to a mesmerizing rock formation resembling an ocean wave frozen in time, and the White Domes Trail, featuring a scenic slot canyon and remnants of an old movie set. For those interested in history, the Atlatl Rock and Mouse's Tank trails showcase petroglyphs that date back more than 2,000 years, providing insight into the region's indigenous cultures.

Camping in Valley of Fire is a unique experience, with two campgrounds offering a total of 72 units, some equipped with shaded tables, grills, and water. The park's facilities are well-maintained, ensuring a comfortable stay amidst the striking desert scenery. Wildlife enthusiasts might spot bighorn sheep, lizards, and a variety of bird species, adding to the park's allure.

Valley of Fire is also known for its vibrant night skies, making it an excellent spot for stargazing. The lack of light pollution allows for clear views of constellations, planets, and the Milky Way. For those looking to escape the hustle and bustle of city life, Valley of Fire State Park provides a serene and awe-inspiring retreat into nature.

2.   Lake Mead National Recreation Area

Lake Mead National Recreation Area, spanning the borders of Nevada and Arizona, is a vast and diverse region encompassing the expansive Lake Mead and Lake Mohave. Created by the construction of the Hoover Dam in 1935, Lake Mead is the largest reservoir in the United States, offering a myriad of recreational opportunities amidst stunning desert landscapes. The area covers approximately 1.5 million acres, featuring a mix of desert, mountains, canyons, and water, making it a prime destination for outdoor enthusiasts.

Boating is one of the most popular activities at Lake Mead, with marinas and boat rental services available for visitors. Whether it's sailing, water skiing, or fishing, the lake's vast expanse provides ample space for water-based adventures. Fishing enthusiasts can expect to catch a variety of species, including striped bass, largemouth bass, and catfish. For those preferring a more relaxed experience, the lake's coves and inlets offer tranquil spots for swimming and picnicking.

Hiking and exploring the surrounding desert terrain is another major draw. Trails like the Historic Railroad Trail offer a glimpse into the area's past, with remnants of the railroad used during the construction of the Hoover Dam. The Black Canyon, located downstream from the dam, is a favorite for kayaking and canoeing, with its dramatic cliffs and hot springs providing a scenic and serene backdrop.

Camping at Lake Mead National Recreation Area ranges from developed campgrounds with amenities to more primitive backcountry sites, catering to different preferences. The region's diverse ecosystems support a wide array of wildlife, including desert bighorn sheep, mule deer, and numerous bird species, making it a great spot for wildlife observation.

The area also holds significant cultural and historical value, with sites like the Hoover Dam and remnants of early Native American habitation offering insights into the region's history. For those seeking a blend of water recreation, desert adventure, and historical exploration, Lake Mead National Recreation Area provides a rich and varied experience.

3. Hoover Dam

Hoover Dam, an engineering marvel located on the border between Nevada and Arizona, stands as a testament to human ingenuity and ambition. Completed in 1935 during the Great Depression, this colossal structure was built to control flooding, provide irrigation water, and generate hydroelectric power. At 726 feet tall and 1,244 feet long, Hoover Dam was the world's tallest dam at the time of its completion and remains an iconic symbol of American engineering.

The construction of Hoover Dam was a monumental task that involved over 21,000 workers and required innovative techniques and machinery. The dam's completion created Lake Mead, the largest reservoir in the United States, which serves as a crucial water source for millions of people in the southwestern United States. The dam itself generates over 4 billion kilowatt-hours of electricity annually, providing power to Nevada, Arizona, and California.

Visitors to Hoover Dam can explore its impressive architecture and learn about its history and construction through guided tours. The Visitor Center offers exhibits and presentations that provide an in-depth look at the dam's significance and the challenges faced during its construction. The Powerplant Tour takes visitors deep inside the dam, where they can see the massive generators in action and gain a better understanding of how hydroelectric power is produced.

Walking across the top of the dam provides stunning views of the Colorado River and the surrounding Black Canyon. The nearby Mike O'Callaghan-Pat Tillman Memorial Bridge, completed in 2010, offers an additional vantage point, allowing visitors to take in panoramic views of the dam and Lake Mead from a height of nearly 900 feet above the river.

Hoover Dam is not only an engineering wonder but also a historical landmark that played a crucial role in the development of the American Southwest. Its construction provided much-needed jobs during the Great Depression and its continued operation supports the region's water and power needs. For anyone interested in history, engineering, or breathtaking scenery, Hoover Dam is a must-visit destination.

4.   Boulder City Historic District

Boulder City Historic District, located in Nevada, is a charming and historically rich area that offers a glimpse into the past with its well-preserved architecture and small-town atmosphere. Established in the early 1930s as a company town for the workers building Hoover Dam, Boulder City was designed to accommodate the thousands of laborers and their families who flocked to the area during the Great Depression. Unlike many other towns that sprang up during this era, Boulder City was meticulously planned with tree-lined streets, parks, and community facilities, creating a pleasant and livable environment.

Walking through the Boulder City Historic District, visitors are transported back in time by the distinctive Mission and Spanish Colonial Revival architecture that characterizes many of the buildings. The Boulder Dam Hotel, built in 1933, is a centerpiece of the district and now houses a museum dedicated to the history of the dam and the town. The hotel, listed on the National Register of Historic Places, was once a luxurious accommodation for visiting dignitaries and remains a popular lodging and dining destination.

The district is also home to numerous shops, galleries, and restaurants that occupy historic buildings, offering a unique shopping and dining experience. Artisan shops, antique stores, and boutiques line the streets, providing a delightful mix of modern and vintage wares. The Boulder City/Hoover Dam Museum, located within the Boulder Dam Hotel, provides an in-depth look at the challenges and triumphs of building Hoover Dam and the impact it had on the local community.

Boulder City's commitment to preserving its heritage is evident in the many events and festivals held throughout the year, celebrating its history and community spirit. The annual Boulder City Art Guild's Art in the Park event attracts artists and visitors from across the region, while the Spring Jamboree and Damboree are popular local festivals featuring parades, live music, and family-friendly activities.

Boulder City Historic District stands as a testament to the enduring legacy of the Hoover Dam project and the community that sprang up around it, making it a must-visit destination for history buffs and those looking to explore the cultural heritage of Nevada.

5.   Clark County Museum

The Clark County Museum, located in Henderson, Nevada, offers visitors a comprehensive look into the rich history of Southern Nevada. Spread across 30 acres, the museum features a variety of exhibits and historical buildings that transport guests back in time, providing a vivid portrayal of the region's past. Established in 1968, the museum has grown to become a key cultural and educational institution in the area.

The museum's indoor exhibit gallery showcases artifacts from prehistoric times to the modern era. Displays include Native American artifacts, mining equipment, and items from the early days of Las Vegas. One of the highlights is the recreated historic street, Heritage Street, which features eight restored buildings from different eras. Visitors can explore these buildings, which include a 1912 railroad cottage, a 1930s-era Boulder City home, and a mid-century modern house, offering a glimpse into daily life during those periods.

The outdoor exhibits are equally captivating. They include the ghost town of Searchlight, a 1900s mining town replica, and an early Las Vegas wedding chapel. The Anna Roberts Parks Exhibit Hall provides detailed displays of the various periods in Clark County's development, from the Native American cultures and early pioneers to the boom of Las Vegas.

Special events and educational programs are regularly held at the museum, making it a lively hub for community engagement. Programs for schools and families include hands-on activities and guided tours that enhance the learning experience.

Nature enthusiasts will appreciate the museum's nature trail, which winds through the desert landscape and features native plants and wildlife. The trail offers a peaceful contrast to the bustling city of Las Vegas and provides a great opportunity for a relaxing walk in a natural setting.

The Clark County Museum is not just a repository of artifacts but a living history experience that brings the past to life. It offers an enriching experience for visitors of all ages, making it a must-visit destination for anyone interested in the history and culture of Southern Nevada.

6.   Lion Habitat Ranch

Lion Habitat Ranch, located in Henderson, Nevada, is a unique wildlife sanctuary that provides a safe haven for lions and other exotic animals. Established in 1989, the ranch originally served as a home for the lions used in the MGM Grand's lion habitat on the Las Vegas Strip. Today, it is dedicated to the care, conservation, and education of these majestic creatures.

The ranch spans over eight acres and is home to more than 40 lions, including several cubs. Visitors can observe these magnificent animals up close in spacious, naturalistic enclosures designed to meet their physical and psychological needs. The ranch's knowledgeable staff offers guided tours, providing insights into the behavior, biology, and conservation of lions. These tours are educational and engaging, allowing guests to learn about the individual personalities and stories of the resident lions.

One of the standout features of Lion Habitat Ranch is its commitment to animal enrichment. The lions are provided with various toys and activities to stimulate their minds and bodies, ensuring they lead healthy and active lives. Visitors can witness these enrichment activities, such as feeding sessions and playtime, which offer an entertaining and educational experience.

In addition to lions, the ranch is home to other exotic animals, including ostriches, emus, and a giraffe named Ozzie, who is known for his painting skills. Ozzie's artwork is available for purchase, with proceeds supporting the ranch's conservation efforts. The presence of these diverse animals adds to the ranch's appeal, making it a fascinating destination for animal lovers.

Lion Habitat Ranch also emphasizes the importance of conservation and animal welfare. It supports various wildlife conservation initiatives and educates the public about the challenges facing wild lion populations. Through its programs and outreach efforts, the ranch aims to inspire a deeper appreciation for wildlife and the need to protect it.

A visit to Lion Habitat Ranch offers a rare opportunity to see lions and other exotic animals in a well-cared-for environment. It is a memorable experience for families, wildlife enthusiasts, and anyone interested in learning more about these incredible creatures and the efforts to conserve them.

7.   Welcome to Fabulous Las Vegas Sign

The "Welcome to Fabulous Las Vegas" sign is an iconic symbol that has welcomed visitors to the city since its installation in 1959. Located at the southern end of the Las Vegas Strip, this historic landmark is more than just a sign; it represents the vibrant, flashy, and glamorous spirit of Las Vegas.

Designed by Betty Willis, a local graphic artist, the sign embodies the Googie architectural style popular in the 1950s and 1960s. This style is characterized by futuristic designs, bold colors, and space-age themes, which perfectly capture the optimistic and extravagant mood of the era. The sign's distinctive diamond shape, adorned with flashing lights and bold lettering, stands 25 feet tall and features a striking combination of neon and incandescent bulbs that glow brightly against the desert sky.

The front of the sign famously reads, "Welcome to Fabulous Las Vegas, Nevada," while the back of the sign bids farewell with the words, "Drive Carefully, Come Back Soon." This double-sided message encapsulates the hospitality and the magnetic allure that draws millions of visitors to Las Vegas every year.

One of the most appealing aspects of the sign is its accessibility. Located on a median strip near the Mandalay Bay Resort, it is easily reachable, and the site includes a small parking lot to accommodate the throngs of tourists who come to take photos. The sign has become a must-visit destination for both first-time visitors and returning tourists, making it one of the most photographed landmarks in the city.

Over the decades, the "Welcome to Fabulous Las Vegas" sign has been more than just a marker; it has become a cultural icon. It appears in countless movies, TV shows, and advertisements, symbolizing the excitement and allure of Las Vegas. The sign has also been featured on memorabilia, souvenirs, and even license plates, further cementing its status as a quintessential representation of the city's identity.

In 2009, the sign was added to the National Register of Historic Places, recognizing its significance in American culture and history.

8.   Pinball Hall of Fame

The Pinball Hall of Fame, located on the Las Vegas Strip, is a paradise for pinball enthusiasts and a nostalgic trip down memory lane for visitors of all ages. Established in 2006 by the Las Vegas Pinball Collectors Club, this unique museum is dedicated to preserving and celebrating the history of pinball machines and arcade games. The museum moved to its current location, a larger and more accessible venue, in 2021, offering an even greater selection of games for visitors to enjoy.

Spanning over 25,000 square feet, the Pinball Hall of Fame houses more than 200 pinball machines, ranging from vintage models from the 1950s to modern machines with intricate themes and advanced technology. The collection is one of the largest and most diverse in the world, featuring machines from iconic manufacturers like Gottlieb, Williams, and Bally. Each machine is meticulously restored and maintained, allowing visitors to experience them in their original glory.

What sets the Pinball Hall of Fame apart is its interactive nature. Unlike traditional museums, visitors are encouraged to play the machines, making it a hands-on experience. The cost to play is affordable, with most machines priced between 25 cents and a dollar, providing hours of entertainment at a low cost. The proceeds from the games are donated to local charities, reflecting the museum's commitment to giving back to the community.

The museum also features a selection of classic arcade games, adding to the nostalgic appeal. From Pac-Man to Space Invaders, visitors can relive the golden age of arcade gaming. The variety of games ensures that there is something for everyone, whether you are a seasoned pinball wizard or a newcomer eager to try your hand at the flippers.

Educational displays and information panels throughout the museum provide context about the history and evolution of pinball. Visitors can learn about the design and mechanics of the machines, as well as the cultural impact of pinball in different eras.

9.   Shark Reef Aquarium at Mandalay Bay

The Shark Reef Aquarium at Mandalay Bay, located in Las Vegas, Nevada, offers an immersive and captivating underwater experience in the heart of the desert. Opened in 2000, this world-class aquarium is home to over 2,000 animals, representing more than 100 species, including sharks, rays, fish, reptiles, and marine invertebrates. It is designed to provide visitors with a deeper understanding and appreciation of marine life and conservation.

The aquarium features 14 exhibits, each meticulously designed to replicate natural habitats. The centerpiece is the 1.3-million-gallon Shipwreck exhibit, which houses various species of sharks, including sand tiger sharks, green sea turtles, and schools of fish. Visitors can walk through a tunnel that runs through the tank, offering a 360-degree view of the aquatic life swimming above and around them. This immersive experience allows guests to feel as though they are part of the underwater world.

In addition to the Shipwreck exhibit, the aquarium includes several other fascinating habitats. The Jungle Temple exhibit features freshwater species and reptiles, including the golden crocodile and Komodo dragon. The Touch Pool allows visitors to have a hands-on encounter with rays, horseshoe crabs, and other friendly marine creatures, providing an interactive and educational experience, especially popular with children.

The Shark Reef Aquarium places a strong emphasis on conservation and education. It participates in various conservation programs and works to raise awareness about the importance of protecting marine ecosystems. Educational displays throughout the aquarium provide information about the animals, their habitats, and the challenges they face in the wild. The aquarium also offers educational programs and behind-the-scenes tours that give visitors a deeper insight into the care and conservation efforts involved in maintaining the exhibits.

One of the unique offerings at Shark Reef is the opportunity to dive with sharks. Certified divers can participate in a guided dive in the Shipwreck exhibit, getting up close and personal with the sharks and other marine life. This once-in-a-lifetime experience provides a thrilling adventure for diving enthusiasts.

10.   T-Mobile Arena

T-Mobile Arena, located on the Las Vegas Strip, is a state-of-the-art multi-purpose venue that has become a premier destination for sports and entertainment since its opening in April 2016. The arena, with a seating capacity of 20,000, hosts a wide variety of events, including concerts, sporting events, award shows, and conventions, making it a central hub of activity in Las Vegas.

The arena is perhaps best known as the home of the NHL's Vegas Golden Knights. The arrival of the Golden Knights in 2017 marked the city's first major professional sports team, and their games have become major events, attracting enthusiastic fans and creating a vibrant, electrifying atmosphere. The team's success, including reaching the Stanley Cup Finals in their inaugural season, has cemented T-Mobile Arena as a key sports venue.

In addition to hockey, T-Mobile Arena hosts major boxing and UFC events, drawing international audiences and top-tier athletes. The venue's versatility allows it to be transformed for basketball, concerts, and other large-scale events, featuring performances by world-renowned artists like Lady Gaga, Elton John, and the Rolling Stones. Its cutting-edge acoustics and modern amenities ensure a high-quality experience for every attendee.

Architecturally, T-Mobile Arena stands out with its sleek, contemporary design and eco-friendly features. It boasts a stunning facade of glass and steel, complemented by an outdoor plaza that hosts pre-event festivities and concerts. The arena's interior is designed for maximum comfort and convenience, offering premium seating options, luxury suites, and a wide range of food and beverage choices.

Sustainability is a key focus at T-Mobile Arena, with features such as water-efficient landscaping, energy-efficient lighting, and a comprehensive recycling program. These efforts have earned the venue LEED Gold certification, demonstrating a commitment to environmental responsibility.

Located at the heart of the Las Vegas Strip, T-Mobile Arena is easily accessible and surrounded by numerous hotels, casinos, and dining options, making it a convenient and attractive destination for both locals and tourists.

11. Eiffel Tower Viewing Deck

The Eiffel Tower Viewing Deck, located at the Paris Las Vegas Hotel and Casino on the Las Vegas Strip, offers visitors a taste of Parisian charm in the heart of Nevada. This half-scale replica of the iconic Parisian landmark stands at 46 stories tall, providing breathtaking panoramic views of the Las Vegas skyline and the surrounding desert landscape.

Completed in 1999, the Eiffel Tower at Paris Las Vegas has become a beloved landmark in its own right, offering an immersive experience that combines the romance and elegance of Paris with the excitement and glamour of Las Vegas. The viewing deck, accessible by a glass elevator ride, is located 460 feet above the ground, providing an ideal vantage point for sightseeing and photography.

From the top, visitors can enjoy stunning views of many of Las Vegas' most famous attractions, including the Bellagio Fountains, the High Roller Observation Wheel, and the glittering expanse of the Strip. The deck is particularly popular at night, when the city is illuminated by countless lights, creating a dazzling spectacle. The Eiffel Tower light show, featuring a choreographed display of twinkling lights, adds to the enchanting ambiance.

The Eiffel Tower Viewing Deck also offers a romantic setting, making it a popular spot for marriage proposals and special celebrations. Its intimate atmosphere and stunning views create a memorable backdrop for these significant moments. For those looking to enhance their experience, the Eiffel Tower Restaurant, located on the 11th floor, provides gourmet French cuisine along with scenic views, offering a perfect blend of fine dining and sightseeing.

The Paris Las Vegas Hotel itself adds to the overall experience, with its Parisian-themed architecture, cobblestone streets, and replicas of other famous French landmarks, such as the Arc de Triomphe and the Louvre. This attention to detail creates an immersive environment that transports visitors to the City of Light.

12.   Bellagio Hotel and Casino

The Bellagio Hotel and Casino, located on the Las Vegas Strip, is an iconic destination renowned for its luxury, elegance, and world-class amenities. Opened in 1998, the Bellagio was inspired by the Lake Como town of Bellagio in Italy and is celebrated for its exquisite design, opulent decor, and exceptional service, setting a high standard for luxury resorts worldwide.

One of the most famous features of the Bellagio is its stunning Fountains of Bellagio. This large, choreographed water fountain set in a man-made lake is a spectacular sight, with water jets shooting up to 460 feet in the air, synchronized to music and lights. The fountain shows are held every 30 minutes in the afternoons and early evenings, and every 15 minutes from 8 p.m. to midnight, drawing crowds who marvel at the intricate performances.

The Bellagio is also home to a wide array of dining options, including several Michelin-starred restaurants. Fine dining establishments like Picasso, which showcases the works of the famous artist, and Le Cirque, known for its French cuisine, offer exceptional culinary experiences. The resort also features more casual dining options, catering to a variety of tastes and preferences.

The Bellagio Conservatory & Botanical Gardens is another highlight, offering a stunning display of seasonal flowers and plants. The garden's exhibits change five times a year, each meticulously designed to celebrate the beauty of nature and reflect the changing seasons and major holidays.

For those seeking entertainment, the Bellagio is home to "O" by Cirque du Soleil, a mesmerizing aquatic-themed show that combines acrobatics, synchronized swimming, and breathtaking stunts. The Bellagio Gallery of Fine Art also offers rotating exhibits of masterpieces from renowned artists, providing a cultural touch to the resort's offerings.

The Bellagio's casino is equally impressive, featuring a wide range of gaming options, from poker and blackjack to slot machines and high-stakes tables. The casino's elegant design and high-end service create a luxurious gaming experience.

13.   Las Vegas Strip

The Las Vegas Strip, a 4.2-mile stretch of Las Vegas Boulevard South, is the heart and soul of the city, renowned for its vibrant energy, luxurious resorts, and endless entertainment options. This iconic roadway is home to many of the world's largest hotels, casinos, and entertainment venues, making it a premier destination for tourists globally.

The Strip's evolution began in the 1940s with the opening of the El Rancho Vegas, the first hotel-casino on what would become the Strip. Since then, the area has transformed into a dazzling spectacle of lights, architecture, and extravagance, attracting over 42 million visitors annually. Each hotel and casino offers a unique theme and experience, contributing to the area's dynamic atmosphere.

Visitors can enjoy an array of world-class entertainment on the Las Vegas Strip. From mesmerizing Cirque du Soleil shows like "O" at the Bellagio and "Mystère" at Treasure Island to concerts by top artists and performances by renowned magicians such as David Copperfield, the Strip offers something for every taste. Its vibrant nightlife, with numerous nightclubs, bars, and lounges, provides endless opportunities for revelry.

The Strip's architecture is striking, featuring iconic landmarks like the pyramid-shaped Luxor Hotel, the Venetian's replica of Venice's Grand Canal, and the Paris Las Vegas's half-scale Eiffel Tower. The Bellagio's dancing fountains, the Mirage's erupting volcano, and the High Roller Observation Wheel add to the visual spectacle.

Dining on the Strip is an experience, with a plethora of restaurants offering cuisine from around the world. Celebrity chefs like Gordon Ramsay, Wolfgang Puck, and Joël Robuchon have established renowned dining establishments here, ensuring culinary enthusiasts are well catered to.

Shopping on the Strip is equally impressive, with luxury malls like The Forum Shops at Caesars Palace, The Shops at Crystals, and Fashion Show Mall offering high-end brands and unique boutiques. These shopping destinations provide a mix of luxury, fashion, and entertainment, making them must-visit spots for fashionistas and shoppers.

14.   Flamingo Wildlife Habitat

The Flamingo Wildlife Habitat, nestled within the Flamingo Las Vegas Hotel and Casino, is a serene oasis amidst the hustle and bustle of the Las Vegas Strip. This 15-acre habitat offers a peaceful retreat with lush gardens, winding pathways, and a variety of exotic animals, providing a unique attraction for visitors seeking a break from the vibrant city life.

The habitat's main attraction is, of course, the Chilean flamingos, whose striking pink plumage adds a splash of color to the verdant surroundings. These elegant birds roam freely within the habitat, allowing guests to observe them up close. The habitat is also home to a diverse array of other wildlife, including swans, ducks, koi fish, turtles, and even rescued pelicans, making it a haven for animal lovers.

One of the standout features of the Flamingo Wildlife Habitat is its commitment to providing a naturalistic environment for its residents. The area is beautifully landscaped with cascading waterfalls, palm trees, and vibrant flowers, creating a tropical paradise in the middle of the desert. The tranquil ponds and streams that meander through the habitat further enhance its serene ambiance.

The habitat is open to the public daily, and admission is free, making it an accessible attraction for visitors of all ages. Informational plaques are placed throughout the habitat, offering educational insights into the various species and their natural behaviors. This educational component, combined with the habitat's beauty, makes it a popular destination for families and nature enthusiasts.

Daily feedings and educational programs provide additional opportunities for guests to learn about the animals and their care. These interactive experiences not only entertain but also foster a greater appreciation for wildlife conservation.

The Flamingo Wildlife Habitat is more than just an attraction; it is a testament to the Flamingo Hotel's rich history and commitment to preserving nature amidst urban development.

15.   High Roller Ferris Wheel

The High Roller Ferris Wheel, located at The LINQ Promenade on the Las Vegas Strip, stands as the world's tallest observation wheel, offering unparalleled views of the city. Opened in March 2014, this impressive structure rises 550 feet into the sky, making it one of the most distinctive landmarks in Las Vegas.

The High Roller features 28 spacious cabins, each capable of holding up to 40 passengers. These cabins are equipped with large glass windows, providing a 360-degree panoramic view of the Strip, the surrounding mountains, and the expansive desert beyond. The cabins are also climate-controlled, ensuring a comfortable ride regardless of the weather.

A full rotation on the High Roller takes approximately 30 minutes, allowing passengers ample time to take in the breathtaking scenery. The experience is further enhanced by an informative audio tour that highlights significant landmarks and offers insights into the history and development of Las Vegas. For those looking for a more personalized experience, private cabins are available for special events, such as weddings, corporate gatherings, and parties.

One of the High Roller's most popular features is its "Happy Half Hour" experience, where guests can enjoy an open bar within the cabin, turning the ride into a unique social event. This option is particularly popular during the evening, when the city lights up in a dazzling display of neon and LED.

The High Roller Ferris Wheel is more than just an observation point; it is a symbol of modern Las Vegas, blending cutting-edge technology with the city's flair for entertainment and luxury. It offers a serene and captivating contrast to the excitement and energy of the Strip below, providing a perfect escape for visitors looking to take in the sights from a different perspective.

As part of The LINQ Promenade, the High Roller is surrounded by a variety of dining, shopping, and entertainment options, making it a convenient and enjoyable addition to any visit to Las Vegas. Whether you're a first-time visitor or a seasoned traveler, a ride on the High Roller Ferris Wheel promises an unforgettable experience and a new way to see the city.

16.   The LINQ Promenade

The LINQ Promenade, located at the heart of the Las Vegas Strip, is a lively and bustling open-air entertainment district that offers a diverse array of attractions, dining, shopping, and nightlife. Opened in 2014 as part of Caesars Entertainment's revitalization project, the Promenade has quickly become a popular destination for both tourists and locals, providing a vibrant and dynamic atmosphere that captures the essence of Las Vegas.

One of the central features of The LINQ Promenade is the High Roller Ferris Wheel, the tallest observation wheel in the world. This iconic attraction offers stunning panoramic views of the city and serves as a focal point around which the Promenade's activities revolve. The High Roller provides an unforgettable experience, especially at night when the city is illuminated in a sea of lights.

The Promenade itself is a pedestrian-friendly street lined with a variety of shops, restaurants, bars, and entertainment venues. Visitors can explore a range of retail options, from trendy boutiques and souvenir shops to specialty stores offering unique finds. The dining scene at The LINQ Promenade is equally diverse, featuring everything from casual eateries and quick bites to upscale restaurants and gourmet dessert shops. Popular spots include Gordon Ramsay Fish & Chips, Chayo Mexican Kitchen + Tequila Bar, and the unique, Instagram-worthy Icebar.

Entertainment is at the core of The LINQ Promenade's appeal. Live performances, street musicians, and various events are frequently held, adding to the lively atmosphere. The Promenade also features distinctive attractions like the VR Adventures virtual reality experience, Fly LINQ Zipline, which offers an exhilarating ride above the Promenade, and the Brooklyn Bowl, a combination of a bowling alley, concert venue, and restaurant.

At night, The LINQ Promenade transforms into a vibrant nightlife destination with an array of bars and clubs offering everything from craft cocktails and beer to live DJ sets and dance floors. Popular spots include O'Sheas Casino, known for its fun and lively atmosphere, and the upscale AmeriCAN Beer & Cocktails.

17.   The Mirage Secret Garden and Dolphin Habitat

The Mirage Secret Garden and Dolphin Habitat, located at The Mirage Hotel and Casino on the Las Vegas Strip, offers visitors a unique opportunity to explore an exotic wildlife sanctuary amidst the glitz and glamour of Las Vegas. Created by famed illusionists Siegfried & Roy, the attraction opened in 1990 and continues to captivate guests with its rare and majestic animals and educational experiences.

The Secret Garden is home to a variety of big cats, including white lions, white tigers, and leopards. These magnificent creatures reside in lush, tropical environments designed to mimic their natural habitats, providing a comfortable and enriching space for them to live and thrive. Visitors can observe these animals up close and learn about their behaviors, conservation status, and the efforts being made to protect them in the wild.

The Dolphin Habitat, a state-of-the-art facility, houses a family of bottlenose dolphins. The habitat includes four connected pools containing over 2.5 million gallons of water, providing ample space for the dolphins to swim and play. Guests can watch the dolphins from various viewing points, both above and below the water, offering a comprehensive view of their graceful movements and playful interactions.

One of the highlights of the Dolphin Habitat is the educational programs offered to visitors. These programs include trainer-led sessions where guests can learn about dolphin care, behavior, and training techniques. The "Trainer for a Day" program allows participants to work alongside the professional staff, gaining hands-on experience in caring for and interacting with the dolphins.

The Mirage Secret Garden and Dolphin Habitat also emphasizes the importance of conservation and education. The attraction supports various wildlife conservation programs and works to raise awareness about the challenges facing endangered species. Informational displays and interactive exhibits provide guests with valuable insights into the importance of wildlife preservation and the role that each individual can play in protecting these incredible animals.

18. The Mirage Volcano

The Mirage Volcano, located in front of The Mirage Hotel and Casino on the Las Vegas Strip, is one of the city's most iconic and enduring attractions. Since its debut in 1989, the volcano has thrilled millions of visitors with its spectacular eruption shows, making it a must-see feature for anyone visiting Las Vegas.

Designed by WET, the creative team behind the Fountains of Bellagio, the Mirage Volcano combines cutting-edge technology with artistic design to create a mesmerizing display of fire, water, and sound. The volcano erupts nightly, with shows typically starting at dusk and occurring every hour until late in the evening. Each eruption lasts several minutes and features a choreographed display of fireballs, pyrotechnics, and cascading water, all set to a dramatic soundtrack composed by Grateful Dead drummer Mickey Hart and Indian tabla virtuoso Zakir Hussain.

The visual effects of the Mirage Volcano are truly stunning. Flames shoot up to 12 feet into the air, while streams of water and bursts of fire illuminate the night sky. The use of advanced lighting and sound technology enhances the experience, creating a sense of realism and immersion that captivates audiences. The volcanic lagoon surrounding the eruption site adds to the spectacle, reflecting the fiery explosions and creating a dynamic, multi-sensory experience.

The Mirage Volcano is not only a visual and auditory feast but also a testament to the innovative spirit of Las Vegas. It was one of the first major free attractions on the Strip and set the standard for the elaborate and entertaining displays that have become synonymous with the city. Its continued popularity speaks to its enduring appeal and the fascination that natural phenomena like volcanoes hold for people of all ages.

In addition to the eruption shows, the area around the Mirage Volcano is a beautiful spot to explore. The lush landscaping, complete with waterfalls and tropical plants, provides a picturesque setting that contrasts with the desert surroundings. Visitors can enjoy a leisurely stroll or take photos with the volcano in the background, capturing memories of their visit to this iconic Las Vegas landmark.

19.   Madame Tussauds Las Vegas

Madame Tussauds Las Vegas, located at The Venetian Resort on the Las Vegas Strip, offers visitors a unique opportunity to get up close and personal with incredibly lifelike wax figures of their favorite celebrities. Since its opening in 1999, this world-renowned wax museum has become a popular attraction, providing an interactive and immersive experience that captures the essence of Las Vegas' entertainment culture.

The museum features over 100 wax figures, meticulously crafted by skilled artists who use detailed measurements and photographs to ensure accuracy. These figures span a variety of categories, including film and television stars, musicians, sports icons, historical figures, and Las Vegas legends. Visitors can pose with wax replicas of iconic figures like Elvis Presley, Frank Sinatra, and modern stars such as Beyoncé and Brad Pitt, creating memorable photo opportunities.

Madame Tussauds Las Vegas is designed to be interactive, allowing guests to engage with the exhibits in fun and creative ways. Unlike traditional museums where touching is prohibited, visitors are encouraged to get close to the figures, strike poses, and even participate in themed sets and activities. The museum's themed zones, such as the Viva Las Vegas area and the Marvel Superheroes 4D Experience, provide immersive environments that enhance the overall experience.

One of the highlights of Madame Tussauds Las Vegas is the Marvel Superheroes 4D Experience, which features wax figures of popular characters like Spider-Man, Iron Man, and Captain America. This section includes a thrilling 4D film experience, complete with special effects such as wind, water, and vibrations, bringing the superhero action to life.

In addition to its permanent exhibits, Madame Tussauds Las Vegas frequently updates its collection and introduces new figures, ensuring that there is always something fresh and exciting for returning visitors. The museum also offers special events and themed nights, adding to its appeal as a dynamic and entertaining destination.

20.   The Sphere

The Sphere, officially known as the MSG Sphere at The Venetian, is a groundbreaking entertainment venue currently under construction on the Las Vegas Strip. Set to open in 2023, this ambitious project promises to revolutionize the live event experience with its cutting-edge technology and innovative design.

The Sphere is being developed by Madison Square Garden Entertainment Corp. and is poised to become one of the most advanced entertainment venues in the world. The venue features a massive spherical structure, measuring 516 feet wide and 366 feet tall, making it one of the largest spherical buildings ever constructed. Its distinctive shape and futuristic design have already made it a landmark on the Las Vegas skyline.

One of the most remarkable features of the Sphere is its state-of-the-art LED exterior, which will cover the entire surface of the building. This high-resolution display will be capable of showing stunning visuals, transforming the Sphere into a giant, dynamic canvas visible from miles away. The interior of the Sphere is equally impressive, with a seating capacity of 17,500 and an advanced audio system designed to provide an immersive and unparalleled sound experience.

The Sphere's interior will also feature the world's largest and highest-resolution LED screen, wrapping around the audience to create a fully immersive visual environment. This 16K screen will provide an incredibly detailed and lifelike viewing experience, enhancing live performances, concerts, and events with unprecedented clarity and realism.

In addition to its technological innovations, the Sphere is designed to offer a superior level of comfort and convenience for attendees. The venue will include a range of amenities, such as luxurious seating, premium food and beverage options, and advanced connectivity features. Its design prioritizes unobstructed views and optimal acoustics, ensuring that every seat in the house provides an exceptional experience.

21. The Venetian Resort Gondola Rides

The Venetian Resort Gondola Rides offer a taste of Venice in the heart of the Las Vegas Strip, providing a unique and romantic experience that transports visitors to the canals of Italy. Located within The Venetian Resort, these gondola rides have been a beloved attraction since the hotel's opening in 1999, enchanting guests with their charm and authenticity.

The gondola rides are available both indoors and outdoors, each offering a distinct and picturesque journey. The indoor gondola ride takes place within the resort's Grand Canal Shoppes, a beautifully designed space that replicates the ambiance of Venice with its cobblestone walkways, arched bridges, and painted sky ceilings that change from dawn to dusk. As guests glide along the canal, they pass by upscale shops, restaurants, and cafes, adding to the enchanting atmosphere.

The outdoor gondola ride offers a different perspective, allowing guests to enjoy the fresh air and stunning views of The Venetian's impressive architecture and the bustling Las Vegas Strip. The ride follows a winding waterway that meanders through lush gardens and under ornate bridges, providing a tranquil escape from the city's hustle and bustle.

Each gondola is expertly navigated by a gondolier, dressed in traditional Venetian attire, who not only steers the boat but also serenades guests with beautiful Italian songs. The gondoliers are known for their vocal talents and engaging personalities, making the ride an entertaining and memorable experience. The serenade adds a romantic touch, making the gondola ride a popular choice for couples and special occasions.

The Venetian Resort Gondola Rides are more than just a novelty; they are a testament to the resort's commitment to authenticity and attention to detail. The gondolas themselves are handcrafted by artisans in Venice, Italy, ensuring that they maintain the same quality and craftsmanship as those found in the city that inspired them.

Whether you choose the indoor or outdoor route, the gondola rides at The Venetian Resort provide a magical and immersive experience that captures the essence of Venice.

22. Adventuredome at Circus Circus

Adventuredome at Circus Circus is a five-acre indoor amusement park located on the Las Vegas Strip, offering a fun-filled destination for families and thrill-seekers. Opened in 1993, Adventuredome is one of the largest indoor theme parks in the United States, featuring a wide range of rides, attractions, and entertainment options that cater to guests of all ages.

The park is housed under a massive glass dome, providing a climate-controlled environment that ensures comfortable conditions year-round. This unique setting allows visitors to enjoy all the excitement of a theme park without worrying about the desert heat or inclement weather.

Adventuredome boasts over 25 rides and attractions, ranging from adrenaline-pumping roller coasters to family-friendly rides. One of the park's standout attractions is the Canyon Blaster, a double-loop, double-corkscrew roller coaster that reaches speeds of up to 55 miles per hour. For those seeking even more thrills, the El Loco coaster offers sharp twists, turns, and a 90-degree drop that delivers an intense ride experience.

In addition to its thrilling coasters, Adventuredome offers a variety of other rides and attractions, including the Disk'O, a spinning ride that swings riders back and forth, and the Sling Shot, which catapults riders straight up into the air. Younger visitors can enjoy gentler rides such as the Circus Carousel, the Frog Hopper, and the Miner Mike mini roller coaster.

The park also features a range of classic midway games, an 18-hole miniature golf course, and a 4D theater that offers immersive movie experiences. For those looking to test their skills, the arcade is packed with video games and redemption games, providing hours of entertainment.

Adventuredome hosts special events and seasonal attractions, such as the Fright Dome Halloween event, which transforms the park into a haunted experience with scare zones, haunted houses, and spooky entertainment.

Overall, Adventuredome at Circus Circus provides a diverse and exciting array of attractions that make it a perfect destination for families and thrill-seekers visiting Las Vegas. Its combination of exhilarating rides, family-friendly activities, and indoor convenience ensures a memorable experience for all who visit.

23.   Zak Bagans' The Haunted

Zak Bagans' The Haunted Museum, located in downtown Las Vegas, offers a spine-chilling experience for those fascinated by the paranormal and the macabre. Opened in 2017 by Zak Bagans, the host of the popular television series "Ghost Adventures," the museum houses an extensive collection of haunted artifacts and oddities, making it a must-visit destination for fans of the supernatural.

The museum is situated in a historic mansion built in 1938, which adds to its eerie atmosphere. The building itself has a reputation for being haunted, with numerous reports of paranormal activity over the years. This chilling backdrop sets the stage for the museum's extensive collection of over 30 themed rooms filled with creepy and curious exhibits.

Visitors to The Haunted Museum can expect to encounter a wide variety of items with dark and mysterious histories. The collection includes everything from haunted dolls and cursed objects to bizarre medical devices and mementos from infamous crime scenes. Some of the most notable exhibits include the Dybbuk Box, a wine cabinet said to be possessed by a malicious spirit, and Dr. Jack Kevorkian's "Death Van," the vehicle used in his assisted suicide practices.

One of the museum's most infamous artifacts is the so-called "Devil's Rocking Chair," which is linked to the infamous case of "The Devil Made Me Do It," a story that inspired a film in "The Conjuring" series. The chair is believed to be cursed, and visitors have reported feeling uneasy or experiencing strange phenomena when near it.

The museum offers guided tours led by knowledgeable staff who provide detailed stories and background information on each artifact. The tours are designed to be both educational and entertaining, with a focus on the eerie and unexplained. For those who are particularly brave, the museum also offers special after-hours flashlight tours that enhance the spooky experience.

Zak Bagans' The Haunted Museum provides a unique and thrilling experience for those interested in the paranormal and the bizarre. Its combination of haunted artifacts, chilling stories, and atmospheric setting makes it a standout attraction in Las Vegas, offering visitors a chance to explore the darker side of the supernatural.

24. The Arts District

The Arts District, located just south of downtown Las Vegas, is a vibrant and eclectic neighborhood that serves as the cultural heart of the city. Also known as "18b," a nod to its original 18-block area, the district has grown to encompass a larger area filled with galleries, studios, shops, and restaurants, creating a lively hub for artists and art enthusiasts alike.

This district is a haven for creativity, with murals and street art adorning many of the buildings, adding a dynamic visual appeal. The area hosts a variety of art galleries and studios where visitors can view and purchase works by local and international artists. Notable galleries include the Arts Factory, a multi-use space that houses galleries, artist studios, and creative businesses, and the Contemporary Arts Center, which showcases contemporary art exhibitions.

The Arts District is also home to numerous unique shops and boutiques that offer a range of handmade goods, vintage clothing, and one-of-a-kind items. These shops provide an excellent opportunity for visitors to find unique souvenirs and gifts while supporting local artisans and businesses.

One of the highlights of the Arts District is the First Friday Art Walk, a monthly event that brings the community together to celebrate art, music, and culture. During this event, galleries and shops stay open late, and the streets come alive with live performances, food trucks, and vendors, creating a festive atmosphere. First Friday attracts thousands of visitors each month, making it one of the most popular cultural events in Las Vegas.

The district also boasts a diverse culinary scene, with a variety of restaurants, cafes, and bars offering everything from gourmet cuisine to casual dining. Many of these establishments feature live music and entertainment, adding to the district's vibrant nightlife.

The Arts District is more than just a collection of galleries and shops; it is a thriving community that celebrates creativity and fosters a sense of cultural connection. Its eclectic mix of art, food, and entertainment makes it a must-visit destination for anyone looking to experience the artistic spirit of Las Vegas.

25. Springs Preserve

Springs Preserve, located just a few miles from the Las Vegas Strip, is a 180-acre cultural and historical attraction dedicated to celebrating the natural and cultural heritage of Las Vegas and the surrounding Mojave Desert. Opened in 2007, Springs Preserve offers a variety of exhibits, gardens, and trails that provide a serene and educational retreat from the city's bustling environment.

The preserve is built around the site of the original Las Vegas Springs, which were a crucial water source for Native American tribes and early settlers. Today, Springs Preserve serves as a living museum, showcasing the history and ecology of the region through interactive exhibits and hands-on activities.

One of the main attractions at Springs Preserve is the Origen Museum, which features exhibits on the natural history of the area, including the geology, flora, and fauna of the Mojave Desert. The museum also highlights the cultural history of Las Vegas, from the Native American inhabitants to the pioneers who settled in the area. Interactive displays and multimedia presentations make the learning experience engaging for visitors of all ages.

The Nevada State Museum, also located within Springs Preserve, offers a comprehensive look at the state's history, including its mining heritage, the construction of the Hoover Dam, and the development of Las Vegas as an entertainment capital. The museum's exhibits include artifacts, photographs, and interactive displays that bring Nevada's rich history to life.

For those interested in nature and the environment, Springs Preserve boasts several beautiful gardens and outdoor exhibits. The Botanical Garden showcases a variety of native and adaptive plants that thrive in the desert climate, while the Desert Living Center focuses on sustainable living practices and green technologies. The preserve's network of trails allows visitors to explore the natural landscape and observe local wildlife, providing a peaceful escape into nature.

26.   Discovery Children's Museum

The Discovery Children's Museum, located in downtown Las Vegas, is a premier destination for families and children, offering a wide range of interactive exhibits and educational programs designed to inspire learning through play. Opened in 1990 and relocated to its current state-of-the-art facility in 2013, the museum provides a dynamic environment where children can explore, discover, and engage in hands-on activities across various disciplines.

The museum spans three floors and features nine themed exhibit galleries that cover a broad spectrum of topics, including science, art, engineering, and culture. Each exhibit is thoughtfully designed to encourage curiosity and creativity, providing children with opportunities to learn through interactive and immersive experiences.

One of the standout exhibits is "Eco City," a miniature city where children can role-play different professions and learn about the importance of sustainability and environmental stewardship. This exhibit includes a grocery store, bank, and construction site, allowing children to explore real-world concepts in a fun and engaging way.

The "Young at Art" gallery encourages artistic expression through a variety of hands-on activities, including painting, sculpture, and digital art. This space allows children to experiment with different mediums and techniques, fostering their creativity and appreciation for the arts.

The "Patents Pending" exhibit focuses on innovation and invention, offering children the chance to explore principles of physics, engineering, and technology. Interactive stations and challenges help children understand concepts such as motion, electricity, and magnetism, sparking their interest in STEM (science, technology, engineering, and mathematics) fields.

Another popular exhibit is "Water World," where children can learn about the properties of water through interactive displays and experiments. This exhibit includes water tables, pumps, and fountains, allowing children to explore concepts such as buoyancy, flow, and conservation in a hands-on environment.

27.   The Smith Center for the Performing Arts

The Smith Center for the Performing Arts, located in downtown Las Vegas, is a world-class performing arts complex that has become a cultural cornerstone of the city since its opening in 2012. The center is dedicated to presenting a diverse range of performances, from Broadway shows and classical music to jazz, dance, and family-friendly productions, making it a premier destination for arts and entertainment in Las Vegas.

The Smith Center is housed in a stunning Art Deco-style building, designed to reflect the architectural heritage of the Hoover Dam. The complex features multiple performance venues, each designed to provide an exceptional experience for both artists and audiences. The centerpiece is Reynolds Hall, a 2,050-seat theater renowned for its superb acoustics and elegant design. Reynolds Hall hosts major Broadway productions, concerts by world-renowned musicians, and performances by the Las Vegas Philharmonic and Nevada Ballet Theatre.

In addition to Reynolds Hall, the Smith Center includes the 258-seat Myron's Cabaret Jazz, an intimate venue that offers a cozy setting for jazz performances, cabaret acts, and smaller-scale productions. The Troesh Studio Theater, a flexible black-box space, accommodates experimental theater, dance, and community events, providing a versatile platform for a variety of artistic expressions.

The Smith Center's commitment to arts education is evident through its extensive outreach programs and partnerships with local schools. The center offers a range of educational initiatives, including student matinees, masterclasses, and workshops, designed to inspire and nurture the next generation of artists and arts enthusiasts. These programs ensure that the performing arts remain accessible to all members of the community, fostering a lifelong appreciation for the arts.

The Smith Center also hosts a variety of special events and festivals throughout the year, further enriching the cultural landscape of Las Vegas. These events, such as the annual Heart of Education Awards, celebrate the achievements of local educators and highlight the importance of arts education in the community.

28.   Downtown Container Park

Downtown Container Park, located in the heart of downtown Las Vegas, is a unique and innovative shopping, dining, and entertainment destination constructed entirely from repurposed shipping containers and modular structures. Opened in 2013 as part of the city's revitalization efforts, Container Park offers a vibrant and family-friendly atmosphere, attracting both locals and tourists with its eclectic mix of businesses and activities.

The centerpiece of Downtown Container Park is its distinctive design, with shipping containers transformed into stylish boutiques, restaurants, and entertainment venues. This creative use of space not only promotes sustainability but also gives the park a modern and trendy aesthetic. The open-air layout, combined with artistic touches and green spaces, creates a welcoming environment that encourages visitors to explore and enjoy.

Container Park features a wide variety of shops, offering everything from handmade jewelry and unique fashion to locally crafted art and home decor. These boutique shops provide a refreshing alternative to the typical retail experience, allowing visitors to discover one-of-a-kind items and support local businesses.

Dining at Container Park is a culinary adventure, with an array of eateries serving diverse cuisines. Options range from gourmet burgers and artisanal pizzas to Asian fusion and Southern comfort food, ensuring that there is something to satisfy every palate. Many of the restaurants feature outdoor seating, allowing guests to enjoy their meals while taking in the lively atmosphere.

Entertainment is a key component of the Container Park experience. The park boasts a central stage that hosts live music performances, outdoor movie screenings, and community events, providing free entertainment for visitors. The interactive playground, complete with a giant treehouse and a 33-foot-tall slide, offers endless fun for children, making Container Park a popular destination for families.

29. Fremont Street Experience

The Fremont Street Experience, located in downtown Las Vegas, is an iconic and vibrant entertainment district that offers a unique blend of history, culture, and modern attractions. Spanning five blocks along Fremont Street, this pedestrian mall is covered by a massive canopy of LED lights, creating a dazzling display that draws visitors from around the world.

The highlight of the Fremont Street Experience is Viva Vision, the world's largest video screen, which stretches 1,500 feet long and 90 feet wide. The canopy features more than 16 million LED lights and a state-of-the-art sound system, providing an immersive visual and auditory experience. Nightly light shows captivate audiences with stunning graphics and synchronized music, transforming the street into a pulsating spectacle of color and sound.

Fremont Street is also known for its eclectic mix of entertainment options. Street performers, live music, and various attractions create a lively atmosphere that keeps the area buzzing with activity. The SlotZilla Zipline, a thrilling ride that sends visitors soaring above the crowds, offers a bird's-eye view of the vibrant scene below. With two levels to choose from, including the higher "Zoomline" which allows riders to fly superhero-style, it's a must-try for adrenaline junkies.

The area is rich in history, featuring some of Las Vegas's oldest and most famous casinos, such as the Golden Nugget and Binion's Gambling Hall. These historic establishments offer a nostalgic glimpse into the city's past, while still providing modern gaming and entertainment options. The Fremont East Entertainment District, just adjacent to the main canopy, boasts a variety of bars, restaurants, and nightclubs, making it a popular spot for nightlife.

Fremont Street Experience also hosts numerous events and festivals throughout the year, including concerts, parades, and cultural celebrations. These events draw diverse crowds and add to the dynamic energy of the area.

Overall, the Fremont Street Experience is a must-visit destination for anyone looking to explore the heart of downtown Las Vegas. Its combination of dazzling light shows, historic charm, and endless entertainment options make it a unique and unforgettable part of any Las Vegas trip.

30.   The Mob Museum

The Mob Museum, officially known as the National Museum of Organized Crime and Law Enforcement, is a captivating attraction located in downtown Las Vegas. Opened in 2012, the museum is housed in the historic former Las Vegas Post Office and Courthouse, a building that dates back to 1933 and is listed on the National Register of Historic Places.

The Mob Museum provides an in-depth look at the history of organized crime in the United States, with a particular focus on its impact on Las Vegas. The museum's exhibits are comprehensive and immersive, combining historical artifacts, interactive displays, and multimedia presentations to tell the story of the mob's rise and fall.

Visitors can explore a wide range of exhibits that cover the origins of organized crime, the notorious figures involved, and the law enforcement efforts to combat it. Key displays include actual weapons used by mobsters, wiretapping equipment, and personal belongings of infamous criminals. One of the museum's most notable artifacts is the blood-stained wall from the St. Valentine's Day Massacre, providing a stark and powerful connection to the violent history of the mob.

Interactive exhibits allow visitors to engage with the content in unique ways. Guests can participate in a simulated FBI firearms training exercise, test their skills in cracking safes, and experience a police lineup. These hands-on activities offer a deeper understanding of the challenges faced by law enforcement in their efforts to dismantle organized crime networks.

The museum also highlights the significant legal and societal changes that resulted from the battle against organized crime. Exhibits on the Kefauver Hearings, which were held in the very courtroom where the museum now stands, demonstrate the pivotal role these events played in exposing and curbing the influence of the mob.

In addition to its permanent exhibits, The Mob Museum hosts special exhibitions, educational programs, and public events that delve into various aspects of crime and law enforcement. The museum's dedication to education and historical accuracy makes it a valuable resource for both locals and tourists.

31.   The Neon Museum

The Neon Museum, located in downtown Las Vegas, is a unique cultural institution dedicated to preserving and showcasing the city's iconic neon signs. Established in 1996, the museum offers visitors a nostalgic journey through the history of Las Vegas, highlighting the artistry and craftsmanship of these luminous landmarks.

The museum's centerpiece is the Neon Boneyard, an outdoor exhibition space that spans over 2.6 acres and features more than 200 unrestored neon signs from some of Las Vegas's most famous casinos, hotels, and businesses. These signs, many of which date back to the mid-20th century, are displayed in various states of repair, providing a fascinating look at the evolution of sign design and technology.

Guided tours of the Neon Boneyard offer an informative and engaging experience, with knowledgeable guides sharing stories and historical context about the signs and the businesses they once adorned. Visitors can learn about the origins of neon lighting, the role of sign designers in shaping the visual identity of Las Vegas, and the cultural significance of these vibrant symbols.

In addition to the Boneyard, the Neon Museum features the North Gallery, which houses additional signs and serves as a venue for special events and exhibitions. The museum also offers a nighttime experience called "Brilliant!" which uses projection mapping and music to bring the signs to life, creating a mesmerizing display that captures the spirit of old Las Vegas.

The Neon Museum is committed to the preservation and restoration of these historic signs. Several signs have been fully restored and are displayed throughout the city, including the iconic "Welcome to Fabulous Las Vegas" sign, which has become a symbol of the city's enduring allure.

The museum also plays an active role in the community, offering educational programs and events that highlight the importance of historical preservation and the artistry of sign-making. Workshops, lectures, and partnerships with local schools and organizations help to foster a greater appreciation for this unique aspect of Las Vegas's heritage.

32. Las Vegas Natural History Museum

The Las Vegas Natural History Museum, located just north of downtown Las Vegas, offers a captivating journey through the natural world, providing educational and engaging exhibits for visitors of all ages. Opened in 1991, the museum is dedicated to inspiring a greater understanding and appreciation of the natural sciences through its diverse and interactive displays.

The museum's exhibits cover a wide range of topics, from prehistoric life to modern ecosystems. One of the highlights is the Dinosaur Exhibit, which features life-sized dinosaur replicas, including a towering Tyrannosaurus rex and a Triceratops. These realistic models, combined with informative displays about paleontology and the Mesozoic era, provide a fascinating look at the giants that once roamed the Earth.

Another major attraction is the International Wildlife Gallery, showcasing a variety of animal dioramas from around the world. This exhibit allows visitors to explore different habitats and learn about the diverse species that inhabit them, from the African savannah to the Arctic tundra. The gallery emphasizes the importance of wildlife conservation and the interconnectedness of global ecosystems.

The Marine Life Gallery offers an immersive underwater experience, featuring aquariums filled with colorful fish, coral reefs, and other marine creatures. Interactive exhibits teach visitors about oceanography, marine biology, and the critical role oceans play in the Earth's environmental health.

The museum also boasts a rich collection of exhibits focused on ancient civilizations. The Treasures of Egypt exhibit transports visitors back to the time of the pharaohs, showcasing authentic artifacts, including mummies, tomb replicas, and hieroglyphs. This exhibit provides insights into the culture, religion, and daily life of ancient Egyptians.

For younger visitors, the Young Scientist Center offers hands-on activities and experiments that make learning about science fun and engaging. This interactive space encourages curiosity and exploration, providing opportunities for children to conduct their own scientific investigations.

33. Old Las Vegas Mormon Fort

Old Las Vegas Mormon Fort, located near downtown Las Vegas, is a historic site that marks the origins of the city. Established in 1855 by Mormon missionaries, the fort is the oldest non-native structure in Nevada and offers a glimpse into the early days of Las Vegas. Today, it is preserved as a state historic park, providing visitors with an opportunity to explore the area's pioneer history and heritage.

The fort was originally constructed by a group of 30 Mormon settlers led by William Bringhurst, who were sent by Brigham Young to establish a mission and waystation along the Old Spanish Trail. The site was chosen for its natural spring, which provided a reliable water source in the arid desert. The settlers built adobe structures and cultivated crops, creating a small but thriving community.

Visitors to Old Las Vegas Mormon Fort can explore the reconstructed adobe buildings and learn about the daily lives of the early settlers. The fort's visitor center features exhibits that detail the history of the mission, the challenges faced by the settlers, and the interactions with Native American tribes in the region. Artifacts, photographs, and interpretive displays provide a comprehensive look at this formative period in Nevada's history.

One of the highlights of the fort is the preserved remnants of the original adobe walls, which offer a tangible connection to the past. The site also includes a replica of the original blacksmith shop, where demonstrations of traditional blacksmithing techniques are often held, providing visitors with an interactive and educational experience.

The surrounding grounds of the fort have been landscaped to reflect the historical environment, with gardens and pathways that highlight the native plants and the agricultural practices of the early settlers. Interpretive signs and guided tours offer additional insights into the site's historical significance and the broader context of western expansion.

Old Las Vegas Mormon Fort hosts a variety of educational programs and events throughout the year, including living history demonstrations, pioneer-themed activities, and cultural celebrations.

34.   Las Vegas Motor Speedway

Las Vegas Motor Speedway (LVMS) is a premier motorsports complex located just 15 miles northeast of the Las Vegas Strip. Spanning over 1,200 acres, LVMS is renowned for hosting a wide range of high-octane events, making it a must-visit destination for racing enthusiasts and thrill-seekers.

Opened in 1972 and extensively renovated in the mid-1990s, the speedway features multiple racing tracks, including a 1.5-mile tri-oval, a 2.4-mile road course, a half-mile dirt track, and a state-of-the-art drag strip. This versatility allows LVMS to accommodate various types of racing, from NASCAR and IndyCar to drag racing and off-road competitions.

The most notable event at LVMS is the annual NASCAR Cup Series weekend, which draws tens of thousands of fans from around the country. The event features the Pennzoil 400, a highly anticipated race that showcases some of the biggest names in motorsports. The speedway's seating capacity of approximately 80,000 ensures that it can accommodate large crowds, providing an electrifying atmosphere for spectators.

In addition to NASCAR, LVMS hosts the NHRA Mello Yello Drag Racing Series, where fans can witness top-fuel dragsters and funny cars reaching speeds of over 300 miles per hour. The drag strip, known as The Strip at Las Vegas Motor Speedway, is one of the premier drag racing facilities in the world, offering thrilling quarter-mile runs and intense competition.

For those looking to experience the thrill of racing firsthand, LVMS offers several driving experiences, including the NASCAR Racing Experience and the Dream Racing Experience. These programs allow participants to drive or ride along in real race cars, providing an adrenaline-pumping adventure that's sure to be memorable.

Beyond racing events, LVMS is also a versatile venue for concerts, festivals, and corporate events. The complex's spacious infield and surrounding areas provide ample space for large gatherings, making it a popular choice for major events like the Electric Daisy Carnival (EDC), one of the largest electronic dance music festivals in the world.

35. Red Rock Canyon National Conservation Area

Red Rock Canyon National Conservation Area, located just 17 miles west of the Las Vegas Strip, offers a stunning natural escape from the city's hustle and bustle. Spanning nearly 200,000 acres, Red Rock Canyon is renowned for its breathtaking landscapes, dramatic rock formations, and abundant recreational opportunities, making it a haven for nature lovers and outdoor enthusiasts.

The area is named for its striking red sandstone formations, which are part of the larger Mojave Desert ecosystem. These formations, some of which are over 250 million years old, create a vibrant and picturesque backdrop that draws photographers, hikers, and sightseers. The Keystone Thrust Fault, a prominent geological feature, provides insight into the region's complex geological history.

Red Rock Canyon features a 13-mile scenic drive that offers panoramic views of the area's diverse landscapes, from towering red cliffs and rugged canyons to expansive desert valleys. Along the drive, there are numerous pullouts and overlooks where visitors can stop to take in the scenery, snap photos, and explore short trails.

The conservation area boasts an extensive network of trails catering to all levels of hikers. Popular hikes include the Calico Tanks Trail, which leads to a natural water tank and offers stunning views of the Las Vegas Valley, and the Ice Box Canyon Trail, known for its cooler temperatures and seasonal waterfalls. Rock climbing is also a major draw, with climbers from around the world coming to tackle the challenging sandstone cliffs.

Wildlife enthusiasts will find a variety of species to observe, including desert bighorn sheep, wild burros, and a diverse array of birdlife. The area's rich flora, featuring plants like Joshua trees, yuccas, and various cacti, adds to the ecological diversity.

The Red Rock Canyon Visitor Center provides educational exhibits, interpretive programs, and information on the area's natural and cultural history. The center's knowledgeable staff can offer tips on hiking, wildlife viewing, and responsible recreation.

36.   Mount Charleston

Mount Charleston, part of the Spring Mountains National Recreation Area and located just 35 miles northwest of Las Vegas, offers a refreshing alpine retreat from the desert heat. Rising to an elevation of 11,916 feet, Mount Charleston, officially named Charleston Peak, is the highest point in southern Nevada and provides a diverse range of outdoor activities throughout the year.

The area is renowned for its stunning scenery, featuring lush forests, rugged cliffs, and scenic vistas. The cooler temperatures and higher elevation create a stark contrast to the surrounding desert, supporting a rich biodiversity that includes ponderosa pines, aspen groves, and a variety of wildflowers. Wildlife is abundant, with opportunities to spot mule deer, wild horses, and a variety of bird species, including the rare Mount Charleston blue butterfly.

Hiking is one of the most popular activities on Mount Charleston, with over 60 miles of trails ranging from easy walks to challenging summit treks. The Mount Charleston National Recreation Trail, also known as the South Loop Trail, is a favorite among hikers seeking to reach the summit. This strenuous hike offers breathtaking views of the surrounding wilderness and, on clear days, extends all the way to the Sierra Nevada.

During the winter months, Mount Charleston transforms into a snowy wonderland, attracting visitors for skiing, snowboarding, and snowshoeing. The Lee Canyon ski area provides groomed slopes for all skill levels, as well as facilities for snow tubing and other winter sports. The area's winter recreation opportunities make it a popular destination for Las Vegas residents and tourists seeking a break from the city's mild winter climate.

Camping is available year-round, with several campgrounds offering sites for tents and RVs. The cooler mountain air and serene forest setting make it an ideal spot for camping, picnicking, and enjoying the natural surroundings. For those preferring more comfort, the Mount Charleston Lodge offers cozy cabins and a restaurant with panoramic views.

Educational programs and guided hikes are offered by the U.S. Forest Service, providing visitors with insights into the area's ecology, geology, and history.

37.   Mount Wilson

Mount Wilson, located in the Spring Mountains of southern Nevada, is a prominent peak that offers outdoor enthusiasts a variety of recreational opportunities and stunning natural beauty. At an elevation of 7,070 feet, Mount Wilson provides a scenic backdrop and a serene escape from the nearby urban areas, including Las Vegas.

The area around Mount Wilson is characterized by its rugged terrain, diverse plant life, and striking geological formations. The mountain's slopes are adorned with a mix of pinyon pines, junipers, and other desert vegetation, creating a unique and picturesque landscape. The region's geology is equally fascinating, with exposed rock formations and outcrops that tell the story of millions of years of geological activity.

Hiking is a popular activity on Mount Wilson, with trails that cater to various skill levels. The Mount Wilson Trail is a favorite among hikers seeking to reach the summit and enjoy panoramic views of the surrounding desert and mountains. The trail winds through a diverse range of habitats, offering opportunities to observe local wildlife and appreciate the area's natural beauty. The summit provides a vantage point with breathtaking views of the Mojave Desert and the distant Las Vegas skyline.

Rock climbing is another major draw for visitors to Mount Wilson. The mountain's rugged cliffs and rock faces offer challenging routes for climbers of all abilities. The area's unique sandstone formations provide a variety of climbing experiences, from traditional crack climbs to more modern sport climbing routes.

Mount Wilson is also a haven for wildlife enthusiasts. The diverse habitats around the mountain support a variety of animal species, including mule deer, bobcats, and a range of birdlife. Bird watchers can spot species such as the red-tailed hawk, golden eagle, and various songbirds, making it a rewarding destination for nature observation.

Made in the USA
Las Vegas, NV
27 December 2024

15476245R00075